I Live in a Beautiful World

I Live in a Beautiful World

Julie Bruns

iUniverse, Inc.
Bloomington

I Live in a Beautiful World

iUniverse books may be ordered through booksellers or by contacting:

iUniverse
1663 Liberty Drive
Bloomington, IN 47403
www.iuniverse.com
1-800-Authors (1-800-288-4677)

Because of the dynamic nature of the Internet, any web addresses or links contained in this book may have changed since publication and may no longer be valid. The views expressed in this work are solely those of the author and do not necessarily reflect the views of the publisher, and the publisher hereby disclaims any responsibility for them.

Any people depicted in stock imagery provided by Thinkstock are models, and such images are being used for illustrative purposes only.

Certain stock imagery © Thinkstock.

ISBN: 978-1-4620-2240-3 (sc)
ISBN: 978-1-4620-2241-0 (hc)
ISBN: 978-1-4620-2242-7 (e)

Library of Congress Control Number: 2011909644

Printed in the United States of America

iUniverse rev. date: 06/03/2011

To Mother on her ninety-second birthday

Contents

My thanks to Mrs. Louise Jones for typing my manuscript.
J. A. B.

1

HOMESTEADING 1932

I always feel a little apologetic about not wanting to be a girl. This could be because ours was a five-girl family, and I had an only brother, two years older than I. With two girls on each side, it seemed only right that there should be two boys in the middle. In my adolescence, girls were supposed to grow gracefully into womanhood. To grow up gracefully was fine, but not for me, because I was not graceful. For this reason, I seemed to fit better with boys. I wanted to go swimming with the gang; I wanted to play marbles with the gang. I was always reminded, "Oh, no. You are a girl." I began to think that it was bad to be a girl; what was wrong with me watching a little old marble game? And suppose I did steal a shot now and then? I was probably not too bad, because finally I seemed to be playing marbles, though I never got to go swimming with the gang; oh, yes, I remember I am a girl, but I was willing to wear a bathing suit.

By the time I was ten years old, Mother and Dad probably realized that it was impossible to keep up in town with a gang the size of theirs, because we moved to the country. There, my brother accepted me; we were inseparable. We practically lived out of doors. We fished by day, and at night, we went raccoon hunting—at first with our small colored neighbors and later alone.

After much dickering, we acquired two hound dogs and a lantern, and we were in business. What we did not know was that raccoon hounds had to first grow up, and then they had to be trained to hunt; instead of our raccoon hounds chasing the raccoon, the raccoon chased our hounds. Finally, when we started to light the lantern, our hounds crawled under the house, and there was no getting them out, so we gave up the business of hunting raccoon for a living.

We never gave up fishing, though, and once in a while, we got enough fish for a nice meal for the whole family. Putting squirmy worms on a hook did not bother me, and taking wiggly fish off didn't, either. I always seemed to be hungry, and the thought of a good meal made me work harder.

We each had a pony. We rode with only a rope, and how we stuck to his back I do not remember; I am sure our legs were not long enough to anchor around his middle.

Texas then was a little wild, and so were we. The land for the four miles from our house to town was cut over and was being farmed. From the back of our house, the timber was dense and was not cut through to Louisiana. It had all manner of wild animals—panthers, wild hogs, wolves, and only the good Lord knows what all. We were supposed to stay out of the timber. At first, "Yes." Later, "No." Mother would say, not beyond such and such tree. For some reason, such and such tree kept moving farther and farther into the tall timber, and one day it happened. We rode right into a bunch of wild hogs. First we chased them, and then they chased us. When we got home, I am sure Mother guessed what we had been doing, because a few days later, a man came over to buy two ponies. We had no ponies, so we went rabbit hunting. My mother prepared rabbit better than any I have ever eaten; she put them into a spicy brew overnight and then baked them in cream. The only reason Dad let us have a gun was because he, too, enjoyed eating this delicious meat.

My father was one who liked change of scenery; we never stayed in one place more than a few years. This time, we again moved to town, now more to the western part of the state. My two older sisters got jobs, and so did my brother. And this was where the first tragedy struck our family; my brother was hurt on the job and died a few days later. My parents were deeply hurt after losing their only boy. But I shall never forgot how lost I was; now I was alone in the middle. I finally came alive the way weeds do when a stone is lifted off them. Now I accepted being a girl, and I went to work in a store. I did not know calico from satin or a sailor from a turban. I finally advanced from a counter hopper to a saleslady. For many years, I earned my living working in a large department store, selling dry goods, ladies' ready-to-wear, pots and pans, and whatnot. I liked my job, for selling goods was right up my alley. But I was about as free as a cow in a well. Day after day, I saw the same faces and the same walls in the same store. I walked through the same streets, always in a hurry and never time for play.

One day, I decided that I had to have a change, so I quit my job and came to Wyoming, where I again took a store job. Sure, the work was the same as I had been doing for so many years, but the people were different, the country was different, and there were so many mountains all around that I was sure in them was much hidden beauty—perhaps for only the wild animals to enjoy. I wanted to explore those God-made mountains; I was sure that in them I could enjoy the feeling of freedom. I could think, relax, and rest. Nature's beauty was everywhere. The more I went out into them, the more I was convinced that there I wanted to build my home.

When I had worked in the same store for eight years, I had a little cash in the bank and what looked like a chance to file a homestead up in those high and rugged mountains that I had learned to love.

Withdrawn lands were reopened to World War I veterans, with leftover lands going to civilians. The location was thirty miles south of Glenrock, Wyoming, and much of the way there was only a cow trail for a road. I knew that I would have to work hard if I expected to make my living on a homestead—much harder than I had ever worked physically in all of my life, and that at the end of a long and hard day, my tired and aching muscles would let me know that it was time to quit. But I would be working for myself, building a home on land that belonged to me. I would be free and out in nature, which I so dearly loved. To me, there is something much more beautiful than just man-made beauty.

And, as I am no exception, I had a dream that someday there would be two of us building a home together, and I had a good idea who would fulfill my dreams. My mind was made up.

I would file a homestead. There was land to be had after all of the veterans were satisfied. Making proof would take more money than I had; therefore, I would have to keep my store job for a while longer. Being a civilian, I would have to put in six months of my time on my homestead out of each year for three successive years. And I would have to have proper improvements before I could make final proof. I would have to have a house built before I could go out to live on my homestead. There were many things I would have to take into consideration—I, a lone woman, starting a new life that I knew nothing about.

Having lived all of my adult life in town, could I adjust myself to this new life? I would be alone. The nights would be dark. I would have no close neighbors. And there would be the mournful song of many a coyote telling me that a storm was approaching. And there would be other animals that I would not see, but they would soon know that I had moved in on their territory. Would they try to harm me? Would I be afraid? My answer was definitely, "No." I would not be afraid.

Starting out on a new venture with a strong determination and an honest heart, how could there possibly be anything to be afraid of? The animals would probably be as afraid of me as I would be of them. We would have to learn to live together. I believe that God protects those who seek his protection. Why would I not be protected one place the same as another? Why could I not make a go of it?

There was a section of land if I wanted it, so I filed a homestead. I made arrangements at the store for the summer off. In the fall, I would be back on the job, and all winter, I would work like a beaver making all of the extra pennies that I could by doing extra work. I arranged to have a house constructed out of green-cut, peeled logs. The bedroom-living room was to be sixteen-by-twenty feet, and the kitchen and breakfast nook was to be ten-by-sixteen feet.

For my cabin site, I selected a valley along a creek, sprinkled with lovely spruce trees from seventy-five to a hundred feet tall, mixed with pine and aspen. About an eighth of a mile downcreek from the cabin location were a series of large beaver dams, and on each side of the creek, there was a mountain ridge. By spring, my cabin would be ready, and I would go up to put in my first six months on my homestead.

I had a Model T coupe with a special mountain axle. That would be my burro. At every opportunity, I had been making and buying things for my new home. Winter was gone, and spring came in a hurry. When time came for me to start up to the mountains, my Model T was simply bulging with supplies.

I set up housekeeping in a hurry. I ate off of boxes. I sat on boxes, and my cupboards were boxes. I had all summer in which to fix up my home. I was having a lot of fun. I did not know for sure why. I suppose it was because I was away from everybody and on my own. I had an independent feeling. Now I did not have to keep in mind that a customer is always right. I did not have to say yes when I meant no. But when I worked, I did my job as my employer wanted it done.

Days simply flew by, but evenings were long and lonely. As soon as darkness came, my new world changed. The nights were frightening—owls hooting, coyotes yapping. But just when I did not think that I could sleep, I slept best, only to be awakened from a deep sleep at the first sign of dawn by the sweet song of a robin coming from a nearby tree. And as soon as daylight came, there were dozen of new songs, and I had to jump out of bed and rush to the window to see my many feathered friends. I would kneel half hanging out of the window, listening to the many beautiful songs all coming from different directions at the same time. The robin was still in the tree, swelling his orange chest, pouring out music so sweet that I wanted to kneel there and listen, even if his song lasted forever. Now again my world was beautiful.

I dressed hurriedly and started walking briskly to the beaver dam to make sure that I missed nothing. My path was bordered on both sides with lovely spruce and pine, their branches spreading over my head, alive with color—red, yellow, orange, blue, black-and-white, gray, and rose.

The sweet music was heavenly. I walked slowly under the canopy like a bride walking to the altar to receive her lifetime mate. The air was filled with sweet music, song, and love. I wanted to walk on and on, forever and ever.

As I approached the beaver dams, more beauty met my eyes. A beautiful morning was reflected in the aquamarine lake. A blue marsh hawk slowly circled overhead, his image swimming in the water. A little sandpiper, at water's edge, curtsied to its mate. A pair of mallards, heads gleaming, emerald, violet, metallic, swam gracefully across the lake. The sun, gold and deep pink, peaked over the mountain, throwing long shadows to my feet. And as the sun became more brilliant by the minute, the shadows backed away from me as though now it was their time to be afraid.

But by noon, we were friends, the shadows and I. We had both moved under the same trees to rest on the soft pine needles, I with my hands under my head for a soft pillow, and the shadows making pretty patterns on the pine needles all around me. I watched the colors in the branches as they passed before my eyes. A black bird in his black and red satin. Tiny flycatcher, soft gray, with little yellow underbodies. A black-and-white woodpecker shimming along a tree trunk, his scarlet beanie flashing like a danger signal at an intersection. Little nuthatches, tan and blue-grey, acrobatically looked for their supply of food, all hopping from branch to branch, all longing for love and mating. Their summer nesting place was again a place of passion and enchantment.

When evening came, I went to the dams to watch the beavers at work. If I sat quietly, I was unnoticed, but should I move about, there was immediately a terrific whomp on the water's surface. All activity stopped, and only the beaver giving the danger signal remained visible, swimming in the lake. He was snorting mad. In giving the signal, he slapped the water with his tail in a terrific *whomp*.

Every day, I saw birds that were new to me. They kept coming steadily. No doubt, some had come hundreds and perhaps thousands of miles to build their homes in my valley, traveling successfully, by day and by night, in stormy weather or on sunny days, with only the sun and stars to guide them, yet always arriving at their summer home on approximately the same date as they had for centuries.

At night, I could hear the mating song of the grouse; their drumming came from an aspen grove only a few feet from my cabin. They seemed to feel protection coming from the cabin, and I was trying to give them the protection that they might be hoping for. One day, I saw a hawk swoop down on them, but before I could get out with my gun, he was gone and had only frightened the grouse, but had I not been on hand, he would have had a grouse dinner, no doubt.

In the daytime, I frequently saw the male grouse puffed out, his bright red comb standing out over his eyes like a posy on an Easter bonnet, the black-and-white feathers on his neck and chest like a lovely lei, while he, unafraid, performed a courtship dance for his lady. The lovely bluebird, so meek, gently chirped now and then, trying to talk a woodpecker out of her house, while her mate, in his blue coat soft as velvet, sat in a nearby tree and occasionally fluttered over to see who occupied the little house over which there seemed to be quite a discrepancy. And purplish-green hummingbirds zoomed around, flashing their brilliance like glistening jewels.

Seldom did I see people. However, one day, while I was in the house hammering away building cupboards out of scraps of lumber leftover from the cabin, I heard a voice outside saying, "Doc! Are there any grouse around here fit to eat?" And a man I had never seen stuck his head into my back door at the same time I stuck my head out of the cupboard that I was building, and for a moment, we just looked at each other.

What he expected to see was not there, and what was there I certainly did not expect to see. Finally, I said, "Yes, there are grouse around here, but if they are good eating, I would not know; besides, being protected by law, I am protecting them with my artillery."

Seeing that I was not Doc, he gently withdrew, and I never saw him again in my vicinity.

It was hard for me to stay in the house with all of the wonders of nature on the outside. I could stay indoors only so long, and again I was out exploring.

In the willows along the creek, gleaming like ornaments on a Christmas tree, were Western tanagers and many warblers in their olive-green and yellow plush softness. A tiny wren, bursting into song, seemed to be trying to outdo many of his larger friends, while a pine squirrel, up in a tree thumping his feet on a branch, chattered as if craving attention. A chipmunk, his tiny plume-like tail arched over his back, sat at my feet and ate a dandelion bud. When clouds dashed overhead, a robin singing his rain song told me to get in dry wood that day, for tomorrow would be wet. A pair of sapsuckers pecked as if driving a nail in a hurry to complete their new home.

When I learned to know the animals that lived around me, I enjoyed walking in the woods. Seeing my approach, the little pine squirrel dashed up into a tree, again in its chatter telling the creatures of the woods to run for cover, for danger might be approaching.

I soon learned the meaning of the many noises as I heard them, knowing that as soon as the chatter started, I would see no more animals. In order to see deer at play, I had to go up on a high point and quietly sit for hours, waiting for them to come out to frolic in the valley below me. When the does came into the valley with their fawns, they ran as if playing tag, and they stood face-to-face as if they were dancing. But if they heard that familiar chatter, they disappeared immediately into the timber. It is amazing how well animals understand one another.

A mother grouse trying to distract attention from her young pretends to be hurt, dragging one wing and running in circles while her babies hide so quickly and so completely that one must stand still for fear of stepping on one. This in itself is proof that they have a wonderful understanding among themselves.

Now, by day, the wildflowers were more beautiful and blended in color with the many birds. Along the creek, moss so green and soft and studded with tiny flowers carpeted the ground as if there especially to await a fairy queen. Butterflies dashed in the sun like confetti at a carnival. The hillsides were soft with purple, lavender, and pink crocuses filled with gold. Later, Mother Nature puts them to sleep and then awakens her heavenly blue lupines and many of her pea family to cover the hillsides with deep rose, soft pink, and yellow. In rocky points where she could not keep her fertile soil, she planted pink, lavender, and white phlox. In dark, woody, moist places, she hid the fairy slipper orchids. Where open marshy meadows were deep pink with shooting stars and bordered by white mariposa lily, the placed her throat lavender and yellow green. And brown-eyed Susans stood tall and lovely.

Throughout summer, the array of color was heavenly. Our first spring flower was what the natives call the grayback, because it pushes through the ground doubled and is gray in color. As it unfolds, there is a cluster of tiny white flowers. The flower head comes first, and later comes the foliage. Throughout the summer, it ramificates. Next came the yellow buttercups, bitterroot, daisy, and delphinium. And the Indian paintbrush was no less beautiful, standing like a flaming torch to color the hillsides with her very special red and yellow flame.

And then came the sheep to pick my lovely flowers. Like the other homesteaders, I had my land leased to sheep people for summer grazing. Many bands of sheep were divided into three classes. First came the choice group. They did what is referred to as picking flowers, because they only take the choice feed. The next class took a little more of the feed, and finally, the last bunch took what was left. Grazing time stretched out over about three months—July, August, and September—as up in our mountains, there is danger of getting snowed in after October. So, stock, as a rule, starts down to lower grazing range in October, until finally, by winter, they have reached home and are on winter feeding grounds where the weather is not so severe.

With the sheep people came the opportunity for me to get a dog. But I would be going back to town for winter. How could I keep a dog and live in an apartment? I could not pass up a good opportunity. I took the dog. I would settle the problem of keeping him in my apartment when I got to it.

He was a beautiful animal, a white collie with a brown spot over one eye. He was in poor condition when I got him. He had been in training for a sheep dog, but due to an overabundance of ambition, he could not be used for that purpose, and that was the only reason he was available to me. He was very shy when I got him, and he seemed afraid of me. He was two years old and much confused, and I was afraid that he would not take to me. Everything had happened to him at one time. He was not permitted to help trail sheep to summer range, but instead was taken to town where his owner lived, and then he was taken to another town where he had to stay for two days before he could be brought up to me.

He seemed heartbroken when he was left up here with me. Perhaps, never having been around a woman, he thought that it was no place for him. I did not have a chance to find out what his name was. I thought that if I could speak his name, he would know that I wanted to be his friend. I called him by every name I could think of. Finally, I thought he responded to the name Teddy, so that became his name. But when I later saw his former owner, I found out his name had been Sausage. What a name for a nice dog! Now he seemed to understand, and in no time, we were the best of friends; he was a wonderful watchdog. Then I felt secure. I could sleep with both my eyes shut. The hoot of an owl or the yap of a coyote did not keep me awake. All summer, I could not find one reason why I should go to town, so all summer I stayed in the mountains.

Among the ex-servicemen who filed homesteads on this reopened land was a very special friend of mine. His land and mine adjoined. When he came out to his homestead, he brought my mail and did my shopping. In return, I looked after his place, since he was working in town. He was Otto J. Bruns, but to me, he was Otto. Otto and I had been going around together for some time, and it was no coincidence that we both decided to file a homestead on adjoining land!

My first summer in the mountains was a busy one, as I was building much of my furniture out of scraps of lumber and, not being a cabinetmaker or even a carpenter, it took much of my time. But little by little, before the summer was over, I had a table and benches in my breakfast nook and some cupboards in my kitchen. And now that I had Teddy, he and I went exploring all over the place, and every day, we went to Otto's place three-quarters of a mile downcreek.

The sheep herdsmen on my place were all vouched for by their boss, but I could not help but be afraid of them. I thought a sheepherder was something a woman was supposed to be afraid of. As soon as darkness came, I was in my cabin with the doors locked, but later, when I found out that one of the boys was the sheep owner's son (who is now a doctor) and all the other men were people like myself, out in the mountains because they loved the freedom of being around nature, I was no longer afraid.

Summer was gone before I knew it; Teddy and I would have to move to town for winter. By now, we were inseparable companions. He took to life in town much better than I had expected he would. At first, he was a little confused, and if he could have talked, I am sure be would have said, "Why did we leave our carefree life that we so much enjoyed?"

Otto had voluntarily offered to keep him in his office during the daytime. This arrangement seemed to suit Teddy fine. By now, he knew that we three belonged together. Otto had a completely furnished house on his homestead, so he hired a man and wife to go up to the mountains as winter caretakers for our two places. There was now a team of workhorses on the place. On nice days, the hired man could keep busy clearing fallen trees and could be getting in winter wood at the same time.

Winter in town was the same as all winters before had been. There was not much one could do on the outside. Snow was almost a daily occurrence. Christmas was just around the corner, and we all tried to put as much into each day as we could for fear that Christmas would catch us unprepared.

On Saturday, I was in the store until nine in the evening. Otto and Teddy were always waiting for me to get off from work. Then we would drive to the restaurant for a cup of coffee and a piece of pie and then maybe a show. If I was in the car, the backseat belonged to Teddy, but if he and Otto went places alone, my place in the front seat was his, where he would sit and always seem so happy that he looked like he was smiling. I would start to the car, and over to the backseat he would go, never once having to be told that I wanted the front seat. Otto ate in the restaurant. I accused him of ordering big steaks just so he could bring Teddy the bone, which Teddy expected every time Otto came out of the restaurant. Teddy and I did not have many steaks at our house in those days. We had to watch our pennies and make the most of the dollars so we could again go to our mountains when spring came. But Otto always saw to it that we had a bone to chew on. To us and all the alley cats around the building, he was known as bighearted Otto. Teddy got to know us so well that he seemed to know the meaning of our every movement. He knew that when I went to work, he had to leave me at the store entrance and go to Otto's office and stay with him until evening, when he would be in front of the store waiting for me to get off from work.

In the evening after a ride or a show, we three went for a few blocks' walk for Teddy's benefit. As Christmas came nearer, we were busier in the store. I had little time in which to dream and plan for next summer, but I had to, because there was much to be done and so little with which to do it. My determination was too strong to be easily upset. I expected to accomplish much during the coming summer.

But this was Christmas, a time for new hope and many blessings. I had been selling merchandise for so many years that the month of December had become very special to me. In December, people are so busy, and little children are so excited and happy, looking at toys in display windows, their little noses flattened against the glass and hoping Old Santa will bring them all that their little hearts wish for, but which is always impossible for the old boy to do.

I loved to sell toys. I could almost see children playing with them on Christmas morning. I remember when I was a little girl, having only one doll. It had a china head, and it was blonde. The body was filled with sawdust. I loved it so much. I wonder what the little girls of today would say if they got a doll like that? I made mud pies and baked them in the sun, and when they were baked, I decorated them with wild red berries that grew in the yard, while my dolly sat on a box watching me work. And I made hats from grapevine leaves; I joined the leaves together with thorns and trimmed them with flowers. And I had a little pig that followed me to church one Sunday morning. But now that all seems so long ago. Still, Christmas is as wonderful today as it was then, only now the real meaning of Christmas is in my heart. When I hear people say that Christmas has lost its appeal, I feel sorry for them; they are not letting in the meaning of Christmas.

As far back as I can remember, I have had little time for play, but my life ambition has been to make people happy and to have a place where people of all ages could enjoy nature as God gave it to us for our enjoyment—where young people from the city could see that milk is produced by a cow and not a milk bottle.

Working in a store, I listen to problems of many parents concerning their vacations. Some places did not take in children; some places were too costly for a family to go to. I wanted to help such people, and I hoped that someday I would have a place where they all could afford and enjoy a vacation together among nature.

Before this dream could become a reality, there would have to be much work done and many sacrifices made, as then I did not have the slightest idea where I would get land for such an enterprise. But now that I had filed a homestead, I had the land; the sacrifices would still have to be made.

When the holidays were over and the people had little for which to come to town, the ranchers from out my way were seldom in town. Winter travel over our roads was always hard. But with a break in the weather, they came out like ants in spring. Some came to town to replenish their exhausted food supplies and to bring in their surplus dairy food products and eggs. Others came because they were tired of mushing snow and looking at cows. But whatever the case, the townspeople were always glad to see them. For some, this meant fresh eggs, milk, and cream. For the merchant, it was a little extra business during a slow season.

For us in the store, this time of year meant inventory, cleaning stock, filling shortages, and buying for spring. It was a nice time of year with salesmen coming around with new merchandise, showing many advanced styles and beautiful things for us to sell. I enjoyed selling hats and dresses. Properly dressed people have confidence in themselves, and, as a rule, they are good humored.

March came, and I started packing my belongings. I was moving for the last time. But this time, moving was harder, as I was giving up my apartment for good. I had occupied it for eight years, and the accumulation was much greater than I had anticipated. I discarded many things, and I took only part of my belongings due to difficult travel.

The last four miles to the place were hectic. The hired man and his wife met me at the ranch four miles down from my place. They came with the team and front-running gear of the wagon, with a three-by-three-foot box on the running gear for the three of us to ride in. By the time I got all of my paraphernalia packed into the box, there was little room left for the three of us. Teddy enjoyed running and playing in the snow after being cooped up all winter. The snow was so deep that the team could hardly make it through. The trip to the place was an adventure.

Every time we went over a bump, somebody fell out. One time we hit something in deep snow that must have been a small mountain. We each grabbed for what we could get hold of to keep from going overboard, but the driver did not make the grab fast enough. I looked up just in time to see him flying through the air, holding the lines, sitting on nothing, driving the team. Finally, he landed in deep snow. I shall never forget how comical he looked flying through the air.

After much flying out and landing in the deep snow and then getting out and parking our carcasses back in the box, we got to the place, and to our surprise, we had no broken bones, but we were covered with snow from head to toe. Just the same, I was at home. There would be no more packing and unpacking, moving up and down. I gave my store job up for good.

I felt the change from a steam-heated building to almost no heat at all, but I felt no ill effects from the sudden change—just a little discomfort. By going out into the snow each day for a while, I soon became accustomed to the cold. This was just the first part of April, and it was a late spring, so the snow was unusually deep for this time of year. There were about three feet of snow on the level, except in places where the wind could sweep, but the drifts were from ten to twelve feet deep.

I had no heat in my room. This part was bad. The bed being in an unheated room all winter, with the temperature much below zero, the mattress seemed to have collected all of the cold, and I was unable to get it warm. I lay in bed the first few nights with my knees doubled up under my chin, shivering like a wet pup. Then I got a bright idea. I put a few rocks in the oven and put them hot into my bed. This helped. After that, I always took a hot rock to bed with me. Teddy, too, felt the sudden change.

I soon found a job for myself. Each day, I went out into the forest, and I cut a few poles so that I could fence in my house. Having sheep on the place, one must have the buildings fenced in. Flies run sheep under cover.

In no time, I was as muscular as Popeye the Sailor Man. Soon the ground began to warm up, and the bottom went out of the snow. On cool days, the crust was strong enough to hold me up, but on warm days, going was really hard. When I broke through, I had to get on my hands and knees and come out gopher-style with goo all over me.

People ask me how I could get around without snowshoes. Never having used them, I could not see how I could get along with them. I would probably keep my feet on top of the snow, but my face would be in it. However, I do not claim to be so dumb that I could not learn to use snowshoes. I figured that I would wait to see how bad winters really were up there. And for some reason, I was having a lot of fun in the deep snow. This was the first time in all of my life that I had been in so much snow. We humans do things that are hard to understand. I left a good job. I had a nice apartment to live in. I did not have to put my feet in snow all winter if I did not want to. The block where I worked and lived had one large building. The first floor had many businesses, including the post office, grocery store, ladies' ready-to-wear and general merchandise, beauty shop, men's clothing, garage, and a gas station

I had hot and cold running water in my apartment, and I cooked with gas. And I came up here to live, where for six months out of a year, every time I stuck my foot out of the house, I was mushing snow. If I wanted heat in my house, I used a wood-burning stove, for which I cut wood much of the time. And I also cooked my food on a wood-burning stove. I went to the Johnnie house in all kinds of weather, because this job one cannot put off. When you gotta go, you gotta go. You don't wait for fair weather. I carried water in a bucket out of a spring, warming it on a stove in a washtub, and I took my Saturday night bath in front of the stove.

During summer, the creek was my bathtub. I could not run to the grocery store every day, and I had to stock up with supplies for six months, at least. If I ran out of things that I was accustomed to having, I had to get along with what I had. And yet, I preferred this kind of life. Why? Because I enjoy being out among nature and seeing God's handiwork. I enjoy working out of doors. I am like an old hen with a bunch of little chickens. I am happy when I am scratching in the dirt. I like putting little seeds into the ground and watching them come up and grow into something big and fine—food for me and my animals. There is only one thing I hope to never see grow—myself growing fat and lazy.

Summer came, and the hired man and his wife went back to town. Teddy and I were again alone, but not as alone as we were the first summer, as now we were doing much exploring, trying to learn everything that we could about our country. And people from town were coming out for a little fishing, hiking, and mountain climbing. I was better acquainted with the people in my vicinity. Otto was up on every possible weekend, as his place was the center of activity. He was having three cabins built where people could live and do their cooking. He started out by having a summer home built on his homestead, but his privacy was to be trampled upon; people wanted to come up as pay guests. So the cabins were built and completely equipped for housekeeping.

I stayed at Otto's place much of the day, doing what I could to make the day pleasant for those who came out for a little recreation. My place was hard to get to by car. I had practically no road to my place. Someday, a road would be built upcreek, but as yet, there was only a sheep trail that I used rather than go the long way around by car.

I had little for which to stay at my place. I had done about everything that I could do, including clearing a garden spot and putting in a garden, which did no good because things froze as soon as they came through the ground, as frost settled down into the valley. I soon found out that I had much to learn about this land of mine.

I had definitely decided to winter in the mountains, so we went to work on a plan so that I would not be in danger of getting completely snowed in. I was told by people who knew that my place would be impossible to get to during deep snow. The plan was that we would get an old man to come up to stay during winter. We decided that I should move into Otto's house. Now that there were three cabins, the old man could live in one and do the chores. I would do the cooking for us both in Otto's house. This house, being so much larger than my cabin, seemed to frighten me especially at night—it cracked so much.

One night, I woke to a most peculiar noise. It sounded like someone was sawing logs. For the life of me, I could not figure it out. I had never heard a noise like that before, and I was not going out to see what was making it. Suppose someone was trying to get into the house. Why should I let him in? As soon as I started walking around in the house, the cutting stopped. I went back to bed, and again it started. By then, I was sure that it was an animal, so I took a stick of stove wood and tapped the wall, and I heard no more noise. In the morning, I found that a porcupine had almost chewed through the door. I had oiled the door with linseed oil. He thought that was good eating.

Besides the team, Otto had a saddle horse on his place. I named her Lady, because she was so pretty. After I moved to Otto's place, I decided to build a small chicken house so that I could have fresh eggs.

There was an ideal location for a small building in some boulders behind the house. So for my brainchild, I selected a place where there would be a windbreak from the west and north. The building was constructed out of small logs. The chinking was clay that I dug out of the creek. For insulation between the double roof and double floor and between the rock wall and the chicken house wall, I used rotten wood, which was so badly decomposed that it was like powder and made wonderful packing. The windows were old ones that someone gave me. The roof was a crazy pattern of scraps of lumber leftover from the cabins and some busted-up boxes. Over that, there was a covering of tarpaper roofing.

In all, the cash output for this building was very small, and when I had it completed, it looked nice, and I was proud of my first log house. I already had a few hens that had been roosting in a large box. As soon as this building began to take shape, they seemed to know that it would be their house. I had no trouble teaching them to live in it.

I was simply bubbling over with excitement over the thought of having a winter to myself. After a busy summer, I had reading and sewing stacked up. My mending, too, was badly neglected. The only time during the summer that I could settle down to inside work was on rainy days, but once in a while, I had to take time out, rain or shine, to put a few patches over places where I was beginning to shine through thin spots. By winter, I was wearing more patches than clothes.

Otto brought up one of the many alley cats that he had been feeding. I called him Skipper. In no time, he and Teddy were the best of friends. They put on show for me in the evenings. Teddy would stretch out on the floor by the heating stove for a nap before going out for the night. Skipper would walk around him, back arched, tail twitching, eyes glistening, and all of a sudden, he would pounce right in the middle of Teddy, pretending to be chewing his middle right in two. He would do this stunt over and over, and Teddy would pay no attention to him, but when Skipper's imagination got the best of him, he bit too hard. Teddy would pounce on Skipper and would give him a little of his own medicine, and I would have to break up the battle royal. Teddy, having his feelings hurt, would want out for the night, and Skipper, having had his fun, was ready for a good nap on the foot of my bed before going out on a hunting spree of his own.

I had the cabin ready for the old gent, and I expected Otto to bring him up at any time, since Otto would probably not be able to make it up to the place in his car much longer, as snow was beginning to fly. In this country, we never know from day to day if the road will be open to car travel. I had my grocery list ready so that Otto could bring what he could of the winter supplies before the snow got too deep. I was like a pack rat getting ready for winter. I never came to the house from a stroll but what I had an armful of wood, it would be nice to have when the snow was too deep to go strolling and picking up dry wood. I had no idea what the winter would be like up here, but I was looking forward to finding out.

Teddy and I were in the yard one day, and he dashed away like a deer up a road to a certain hill where he always met Otto. We named this hill Teddy's Hill. From there, he always got a ride home. I knew why he dashed away in such a hurry. Otto was coming. I dashed, too, but I went into the house to brush my hair and put on a face. It had been a long time since I had seen Otto.

When he drove into the yard, there I was all prettied up and as though I did not know that he was coming up. But on the inside of me, oh, golly gee, I was happy! We three were always happy when we were together. Otto and I always had so much to talk about, and he had so little time to stay. It was always I who did most of the talking. I never could get everything said in the short time that Otto was up here. The big hand on the clock moved much too fast. While Otto and Teddy took a quick but short hike, I prepared lunch for Otto. I did not stop talking long enough to eat. That I could do when Otto was gone. Otto found an old man who would like to stay in the mountains during winter.

He would bring the old gent on his next trip. If we had snow in the meantime, he would not try to come up to the place in his car. I should meet him at the ranch with the team and front-running gear. The snow was getting a little too deep for the car, but a day or two of the sun would again open the road. Teddy and I went to Teddy's Hill with Otto; standing on a windy ridge, we parted with a warm kiss. Otto started down the long hill; we watched him disappear into the distance before starting back home. We never knew when he would be back up. His was a twenty-four-hours-a-day job; for this reason, he did not have long to stay when he came up. When Teddy and I got back home, the house seemed too quiet, but the buzz from all of the talking that I had done still rang in my ears.

But, goodness! I'd forgotten to ask Otto how to harness and hook up the team should I have to meet him at the ranch. They had not been in the harness all summer. The only time I saw them hooked up was last spring when I came up. I did not know what side each horse worked on. I was sure that there was a set rule for this. I thought, "If I do things wrong, I may have a runaway." After resting all summer, the horses would no doubt be frisky. Oh, well; I had all week to figure it out.

But Sunday came, and I did not know any more than I knew a week earlier. I thought, "If only I could remember how this outfit was assembled last spring when I came up." One horse was large, and the other one was much smaller. I thought, "Now, let's see, if I were a big, fat horse, what side would I want to work on? Or, would I want to work at all? And if I did work, would I be a jackass, or would I still be a horse?" The traces had to be hooked short enough so that the tongue could not drop down. "I guess I'm not all dumb," I thought. "I seem to know this much." It was important business that I get these horses and this snow buggy put together right. How would I know if I had put it together right? Then I remembered one thing. When one rides in a horse cart, the horse's tail is always in one's face. Phew! And that's in one's face always, too. So, heels to the back, hossie, and head down so that I can put this gap-stop in your mouth. "Down, down, I said, not up. Now, how do I fasten this girdle? I cannot get underneath you. Goodness, there is a lot of you under here. Now will I ever reach the other side? Oh, wait, you are supposed to have a collar on first. And there is something that fits on your big fat hiney; I don't think this harness is all here."

I remember that I harnessed a buggy horse for my dad when I was a kid no bigger than a pea pod. I know that harness had two bridles. One gap-stop was put into the horse's mouth and the other one under his tail. Oh, well, maybe horses are like people nowadays. They just don't wear as many clothes as they did when I was a kid. My, the good old days—even horses had pride. I remember that, when I would try to put the bridle on the horse's head, I had to stand on a box. I would scramble up on the box, bridle in hand, and by the time I was all set to put the bridle on the horse, invariably he had the wrong end to me, or I had the wrong bridle.

"Well, that's that, you are harnessed, I hope. Now if only I can do as well on your partner. Now, what about this mess? These things are supposed to be the lines. They have too many ends. Two long ends, and two short ends. I guess they ran out of leather when they made these things, so they cut two ends short. I think I will just tie you horses together. I don't seem to be able to find heads or tails to these lines." No, I cannot tie them together. I have to drive these poopers. Oh, now I know. Cross cross, so that's the why of two long ends and two short ends. Now, the tongue goes into the breast yoke, and the traces to the riggings go back here.

Brother, brother! I hope I did this right. Well, Teddy, we are ready to go as soon as I park my carcass into this three-by-three-foot box. Toot-tootle, here we go. What do you know? I haven't shifted gears, and already we are rolling. This must be fluid drive. I don't think these horses need me to drive them. They seem to know what to do better than I do. If they know anything that horses are supposed to do, they know more than I do. Hey, you steeplechasers, didn't you see that big rock? Just because I hand you a bouquet, you don't have to go off the road. You almost turned us over. You are supposed to stay in the road. That's why we have roads. Hap! Hold it, I almost got it this time. There is something wrong with this setup. I seem to be too close to you, whistle-breeches. If this keeps up, by the time we get to the ranch, this box will look like you poopers were sitting in it, and I won't smell like Tabu.

Why? All this high-kikas-of-the-pocus, anyway? I wonder if Otto will know this is horse perfume when I get to the ranch? I am sure that I will not smell like a rose.

My timing was good. We all got to the ranch at about the same time. The old gent brought up his dog, Andy. He relayed to the horse cart, and my horse troubles were over. I hoped that the old gent knew more about horses than I did, for they would have to be undressed when we got home.

The trip was uneventful, except for a few dogfights. Andy was as wonderful to the old gent as Teddy was to me, or maybe even more so, if such thing were possible. Andy once saved the old gent's life when his house caught fire; Andy went into the old gent's room and woke him up just in time so that he could get out before the roof caved in. One can never repay a dog for a deed as noble as that. All of the affection a person can give in a lifetime is not enough. I have a deep feeling for all animals, but I think a dog has a deeper feeling for his master than people have for each other.

Coming up, I rode in the box backward with my feet hanging out. The old gent had my place in the front. Every once in a while, I heard him cough, and I thought, "Brother, I know what you mean." It did not take him and his dog long to get settled in his cabin. They seemed very happy to be living together. The place being new to the old gent, he had a difficult time finding the water hole and wood, as by now, everything was getting drifted in. He finally got accustomed to taking a shovel when he went after wood or water. He had very little to do except take care of the horses and do the few other chores. He passed the rest of his time reading.

I had time to catch up on my much-neglected reading, sewing, and mending. Andy and Teddy were in each other's hair constantly. Andy was supposed to live in the cabin, and Teddy did not want him around the house.

Skipper took up for Teddy, and right in the middle of a fight, he would jump on top of Andy's back and ride him all the way to the cabin, chewing and clawing all the way.

The old gent was always afraid that he would run out of tobacco, and he made it a point to tell me that if he had no tobacco, he would die. I guess he wanted to make sure that I would put in an extra supply, but since I did not use it, I figured he could look after his own tobacco supply.

Otto came up whenever he could make it through to the ranch in his car. From there, he walked up. He always came up with a sack on his back filled with goodies for us all—and best of all, a handful of letters for me. Not having a radio or a phone, mail was always welcome. Otto thought he would bring up another man before the snow got too deep. There were many trees obstructing the beautiful scenery around that caught snow and drifted it into the yard. He wanted them cleared out and cut up into stove wood for winter. To keep two houses warm all winter would take a lot of wood. The old gent was very much in agreement with Otto on the need of another man and said that, by all means, he should occupy the cabin with him. If he came up really soon, they could do much work before winter really set in. He was putting in one word for the tree chopping project and two for himself. The old gent had been accustomed to sitting on a street bench and visiting with his friends. To be isolated in a cabin with only his dog turned out to be too much for him.

Before Otto left, he came in to tell me that he thought he would bring the tree chopper on his next trip up, and he would also bring up an additional supply of food. I always reminded him, before he left, to be sure to check on the old gent's tobacco and what other things he might need. Otto's routine was always the same; when he came up, he dashed around like a deer to check on things. Then he hurriedly ate, and before I knew it, he was gone.

I was glad that there would be another man on the place, that the two could pass the time of day together, and that I would not have to worry about the old gent running out of tobacco. It meant more work for me, as I would have to cook for two men, two dogs, a cat, and for myself. But to see how happy the old gent was over the prospect of having company was worth all of the extra work of cooking a little more food. Now, when Otto came up, he left the things that he could not bring up in his pack sack on his back at the ranch. Later, one of us went down on Lady after them.

On one such trip, we had a quarter of fresh beef and many other supplies, which we hauled up with the tear and snow buggy, as now the front-running gear had been christened. Now that the weather was getting very cold, we had to pick a nice day to haul up perishable food. We hung most of it in an unheated room, and in no time, it was frozen solid. When I wanted meat to cook, I had to get the old gent to chop some with an axe.

When Otto brought the tree chopper up, they had to walk from the ranch, each with a pack on his back. When the old gent saw them, he was as happy as a child with a lollipop. They were both tired and hungry when they got up to the place, so again, I hurriedly prepared lunch while they visited in the cabin. After lunch, Otto pointed out a routine to the men, and he was again gone.

I was happy over the fresh meat; having two men to feed would take more food. They would not necessarily have to have a big variety, but a change once in a while was a welcome treat.

My hens were really repaying me for their nice house. Eighteen hens kept me well supplied with eggs, and were the eggs good! The next day, as soon as breakfast was over, both men went out to chop trees. It looked so interesting to me that I wanted to go out and trim off the small branches and burn them. A fire out there in the glistening snow would be beautiful with the blue smoke going straight up to the sky. I could send a message to my lover. I wonder if Indian lovers ever sent smoke love messages? They had, no doubt, some way of letting the little lady know that they would be around. I know they lived in our valley many years ago. This was, no doubt, their summer home and playground when their winter camp was down on the Platte River.

Game then moved like it does now. Things were made to order for the Indian. He did not have to stay on the hot flats during the summer or up in the mountains during winter where the snow got so deep that he or his food supply could not move around freely. They all moved with the seasons. Boundary lines meant nothing in those days, but now we must observe them. I think it wonderful how well the Indian was able to live off of the land. He recognized medicinal vegetation wherever he lived, and he learned to use them efficiently. Animals are like the Indian—or it may be that the Indian learned through observation of the animal, how to make use of resources within his territory.

Before the day was over, it began to get very cold, and by night, everything was cracking from the sudden drop in temperature. In the night, I was awakened by noises. To me, it seemed there was too much of this noise—this terrific cracking of logs—almost like gunshots. At times, the cracking shook the house.

For a while, everything was still, and I went back to sleep, but in no time, I was awakened, and the logs cracked repeatedly. I knew this was caused by a sudden drop in temperature, but how much it had to drop to make this much noise, I did not know. I could hardly wait for daylight to come. I seemed to be getting cold in bed after sleeping warmly all night, and this had never happened before.

Morning finally did come, and I hurriedly started fires in both stoves. I know it was unusually cold. Frost stood out on everything in the house, and it was so thick on the windows that I could not see out. All of the cracks in the boards and logs looked like they were stuffed with down.

I dressed in a hurry and dashed out on the porch to look at the thermometer. I looked, and I looked again, but there was no mercury visible. I thought, "Gosh, what went wrong with this thing? Is the mercury stuck, jammed, or what?" There was nothing wrong. It had only gone its limit—fifty degrees below zero. Now I wonder how much lower it would have gone if it could have gone lower? I had no way of telling. This was the only thermometer I had. I am under the impression that in Yellowstone Park at that time, the temperature was fifty-nine degrees below zero.

Up here, it was dreadfully cold. As the men came out of the cabin, I called to them to take a look at the thermometer. They took a look, and one said, "This thing has no mercury in it."

I said, "It stuck at fifty below zero, and that's as far as it can go."

One of them said, "My gawd, how will we chop trees today?"

And I said, "I think you will do well to keep from freezing in your cabin."

He said, "I will see how I feel after I have a cup of hot coffee."

But the coffee was not enough. I was afraid my chickens would be frozen. I put on a kettle of potatoes for their breakfast. A hot meal and a drink of warm water would help to thaw them out; on a morning like this, they would need special attention. I did not go to the chicken house until after we were finished with our breakfast.

Upon my arrival there, I expected to find the chickens stiff from the intense cold, but to my surprise, they were singing when I walked in. They only had their comb tips frozen; my work to insulate the chicken house paid off.

I shall always remember that heavenly morning. The sun looked like someone was slowly pushing up a huge rose. The reflection on the frosted trees made them look like they were studded with all of the precious stones—diamonds, rubies, and emeralds. A queen was never adorned in more beautiful jewels. On the ground, the frost stood up about three inches thick, patterned like fern and fine lace. One can only see beauty like this on an arctic morning. I wanted to stay outside and forever feast my eyes on this nature's beauty, but the cold was so intense that after only a few minutes outside, I could not gesture with my face. It felt stiff as if mud had dried on it. Suddenly, I realized that my face was freezing.

On the trees, each pine needle was individually coated with frost. The trees all looked like they had long whiskers. The ice on the creek was cracking as if someone had put a explosives under them. The limbs on green trees snapped under the least pressure. Even the fire in the cookstove seemed to feel the cold. It just did not seem to have any heat. I put the dishes we were to eat from into the oven to heat so that the food would not freeze on them while we were eating. Cups froze to the saucers as soon as we emptied them. In the house, each nail head wore a white cap. Wherever the cold air came in through cracks, there was glistening beauty. The heat from the stove had no effect on the frost. The poor water bucket bulged on all sides. I had to chop the ice in it with a chisel and hammer. When I saw how low the temperature was, I started putting on more clothes until I had on so many things that I could hardly waddle.

I had on my galoshes, mittens, and scotch cap pulled down over my ears, and I ate breakfast wearing all of this paraphernalia. I felt like I was freezing to my chair. Once I almost fried a mitten in place of a pancake, but if I had, I don't think anybody would have known the difference. We were all so cold that we did not know what we were eating. I was worried about the horses. I asked the men if they thought their ears would freeze. They laughed and said that they had never heard of such a thing. The brown horses were gray; each hair was covered with frost. They were running and playing so that they could forget the cold. The night—like the morning—was wonderfully beautiful.

I stood outside looking at the dazzling brilliance all around me. The stars seemed to be dancing and winking at me from a clear black sky, flashing and sparkling in a brilliant night. Bucks Peak stood magnificently beneath a glittering moon. Frosted trees again sparkled in their elegance; they stood like a queen on her throne. As I walked over the frozen ground, it made music under my feet. I could not make up my mind if the morning was more magnificent or if now I preferred the beauty of an artic night. I stood, unconscious of the cold, when I suddenly realized that I was almost too stiff to move my feet. I had to go into the house and perhaps never again see a night so beautiful.

The next morning, the temperature was up to twenty-seven degrees below zero, and a high wind was blowing. To me, this morning was the colder of the two. After December 21, we were out of the pit, and days were getting longer. I felt like I was going up a ladder. Sometimes Otto made it up, but he said that the last four miles were getting too hard to walk.

He thought he might as well take the tree chopper down, as he did not think he would be up again until spring. After the first of the year, snow really set in. The old gent began to worry about his tobacco supply. I was worried about what I would do should something happen to him. Would I have to put him into cold storage until spring? We had three feet of snow in twenty-four hours. The old gent started pacing the floor.

As soon as the snow was crusted so that he could walk on top of it, he and his dog pulled out. He walked a ways down the creek and hopped a sled ride into town. Teddy and I would have to face alone whatever came from now on.

Teddy had a swollen place on his temple. It seemed to hurt him. I'd had the old gent take a letter to Otto for me. I told Otto that I thought Teddy should be taken to a doctor, for I was afraid of infection in his head. I had no way to care for him should this turn out to be something serious. Now that we were alone, he seemed to feel more responsibility. Each evening, he made the rounds as though he were checking on everything. Having him was almost like having a person around, and in many ways, he was better than many people. How many people would feel a responsibility with a pain as terrific as he must have had? But he went on never making a sound or showing any sign of discomfort. Animals suffer more silently than do people.

Snow kept coming, but now only a few inches at a time. My trails on the crusted snow were now constantly covered with fresh snow, but to find them, all I had to do was tell Teddy where I wanted to go. He could always walk in the new fluffy snow over the hard trail that was underneath. I know his poor head was painful to him, for now it was more swollen. He kept rubbing his head in the snow, trying to break the abscess.

One day, I decided to walk down to the ranch to see if the folks there could tell me what to do for Teddy. The snow was crusted. I was sure that I could stay on top of it, but the horse would break through. Going for a horseback ride in deep snow would be almost impossible, and with my feeling for animals, I would not enjoy riding under such circumstances.

I would take a letter down for Otto. The folks would mail it for me. I would ask him again to come for Teddy if he could possibly get through. Teddy went down with me. He would have gone if he had been half dead.

Going down was not bad. We stayed on top of the crusted snow all the way, and it only took us one hour to walk the four miles, but going was all downhill. The trip home would take longer.

The folks at the ranch were glad to see me. We had a nice, but short, visit. I told them about Teddy having a bad temple. I wanted to know what they thought I should do.

They said he had an abscess, but they thought he could break it as he was doing, and he would be all right. Clouds gathered and stood out like huge balls of cotton candy, and owls hooted in midday. The missus said that we would have a bad storm within twenty-four hours. I asked them if they would mail my letter, and then I bid them good-bye and started back home in a hurry. All the way home, I watched the clouds.

The mountains around me appeared, vanished, and reappeared through flying clouds. Cumulonimbus clouds stood out like frosting heaped up on a huge cake and seemed to be so near that to touch them, all I had to do was raise my hand. But that downy elegance was not near, and it was not by any means standing still. Gleaming brilliant in the sunlight and then ugly deep violet, indigo, and muddy under passing clouds, churning like ocean waves being whipped by a gale, the clouds were unmistakable evidence of a bad storm. I was so busy watching the clouds that I did not realize that I had been walking dreadfully fast until I began to come up the last hill.

But I had to keep going. I had no time to lose. When I got home, I would have to get in all of the wood that I could possibly find and fill all water buckets. The water hole would be hard to find should we get an unusual amount of snow. I had been digging wood and water out for many days, and no more I had dug them out when again everything drifted under.

When I got home, after walking eight miles, I was tired and felt very hollow inside, but I could not stop to eat. Darkness on a day like this would come quickly. Teddy was right on my heels. He, too, seemed to sense the storm. Before darkness came, the sky took on a new look. It now looked like someone had brushed all of the roughness into a smooth, creamy softness, and there was an absolute stillness. It began to snow. As I worked, the downy elegance softly settled on my dark coat sleeve, each flake a fairy fern. They stuck and lay where they fell, each in more splendor than the one before; my trails, feathery soft, filled inch by inch, full at last. I went to bed, because there was nothing else I could do, but I could not sleep. I felt as if I would suffocate. I tried to look out through a window.

What I could see looked like someone pouring flour out of a sack (like I had once watched in a flour mill). I thought daylight would never come. I was frightened, because I could not see what was really happening. Were we being buried alive? What were the animals doing on a night like this? Finally, I fell into a deep sleep from fatigue, only to wake in the morning to a sea of whiteness.

The pole fence around the yard was not there, and many other landmarks had completely vanished, but snow kept coming. Everything was blotted out, and I felt like someone had drawn a huge curtain around me. I remembered the ugly flying clouds of the day before. I wondered if I could get out to where I kept the feed. I had to care for the horses and chickens. Somehow, I got to the cabin and to the chicken house, a total distance of about two thousand feet, but I could do no more. I spent the day within four walls of the house. All sound seem muffled.

Teddy and Skipper seemed to read my feelings. Skipper occasionally came to me and rubbed on my legs, purring as if trying to say, "Everything will come out all right."

I had to be very careful with my scant wood supply. I probably would have enough until it quit snowing. For three days and nights, Mother Nature kept grinding away at her huge snow sifter. At times, it sifted; at times, it poured. When it finally quit, we had five feet of fresh snow on top of the old snow. This was not dry winter snow that puffs up like down, but heavy spring snow filled with water. I was worried that the house roof would cave in under the terrific weight. The living room roof, having a thirty-five-foot span, was sagging under the strain.

As soon as the snow let up a little, I got up on the roof and started pushing snow, but I had only started, and the snow was even with the roof. I could push no more. Now, if I took any more off, I would have to use a shovel and throw it out of my way. I had shoveled so much getting to the chicken house and to the cabin where I kept the feed. To shovel the snow from the roof would be an ordeal of strength and endurance that I could not seem to muster, so I had to give up unfinished, but that snow I did take off helped to relieve the strain on the roof. I still had many places to shovel so that the animals and I could survive. The chicken house was completely covered. I had only shoveled snow away from the door so that I could go in to feed the chickens and to gather what eggs there were, but little by little, I would have to do more. They would have to have light so that they could see to eat.

I cleared the snow from one window. That would do for a while. Teddy, with all the pain and making no fuss whatever, leaped through the deep snow, making trail for me in his own way. He was always ready to be helpful. The horses also helped to make trail, but their trails all zigzagged and were of little help, leading to no place in particular.

Lady, the saddle horse, was expecting a baby. Babies always come in a storm. I felt a douby of hers being an exception. I would have to get ready for the blessed event, but how? There was a cabin under construction, all finished but the floor. That would be Lady's maternity house. I tried to put her in there, but she said, "Oh, no you don't." We went around and around for a while, and she gave in after I promised that I would not close the door on her. I nailed boards across the door opening so that she could fraternize with the team horses. They, too, were lady horses; I think they were in sympathy with her.

The next morning, she had her baby, a little bay colt. His tail was so long that I called him Felix. I did not let Lady out the first day after her baby came; I took feed and water to her. I did not know what would happen to little Felix if he got into the deep snow. It took me all day to do the necessary work, as it was almost impossible for me to get around in the snow.

My five feet three inches would have gone out of sight had I missed the old trail under all of the new snow. I now could find the trail only by probing with a long stick. Going was hard and slow. Each night, my legs and arms felt as though they were chunks of lead. If my faith had not been strong and my muscles hard, I could not have carried on. Just when I was so tired that I did not think I could go another step, I seemed to get my second wind. Each night, I prayed for strength and courage.

I felt certain that I could make it if we did not have another storm right after this one, as in this country, one is certain of nothing. Day after day, I took care of my animals, many times myself skipping a meal. This was no time to pity myself. I had to take every precaution not to get hurt or sick. Outside of that, I was better off not to think too much about myself. Should something happen to me, we could all be dead before someone came. I felt like I was in a prison. I lived within the space of two rooms and a few zigzagged trails, but I could always look up. Now the sky was again a beautiful blue.

In a situation like this, one feels so helpless. One tries so hard to go through all of the whiteness, but it is almost impossible to push through it, and suddenly one realizes one's smallness in comparison with the greatness of a Divine Being. The soul, too, goes through a test.

Poor Skipper, too, was helpless in the snow. He would jump into it and go completely out of sight, and all that I could see was snow moving. He did not play with Teddy; he seemed to sense Teddy's pain. Now I had to let Lady out for a little exercise and a drink. Little Felix did not know what all of the whiteness was. If he got off the trail, all I could see was turbulence under the snow. Those wobbly legs did not want to stay put.

Most all day, I looked like something the cat dragged in. I did not have to worry about unexpected company, but I would have welcomed even a ghost. There was no use building up hopes for company. I knew that it was impossible for anyone to make it up for a week or two. All would depend on how fast the snow thawed. There was one encouragement. The sun was now high enough to put out heat; if it could ever shine, it would settle the snow. I was not too sure that my feed would hold out until the snow thawed and the horses could go out and do a little grubbing for themselves, but by rationing them, I felt sure that I would have enough feed to keep them going for two more weeks, and surely by then, the snow would be thawed enough so that they could do a little grazing. I could not let myself think of another possible storm.

For two weeks, each day was the same as the one before. Each day, I did a little extra shoveling. One by one, things began to stick out of the snow. After a week of shoveling, I had the chicken house shoveled out and a little yard where the chickens could get a little exercise and sunshine. They went to work as soon as they saw a little bare ground, scratching and pulling out big, fat earthworms.

Next, I uncovered what little wood I had cut, but it was too water-soaked to burn. It would first have to dry out. The sun on the sea of whiteness was so brilliant that it was blinding, but the animals were simply soaking it in. The chickens lied on the wet ground, one wing and leg outstretched, feathers ruffled all over their bodies, trying to soak in all of the sunshine possible after days of being cooped up and much of the time with light enough only to pick up a little food. The birds were so hungry that they came right up to me for a few crumbs. I managed to get a long post, which I set into the ground, and I nailed a shallow box on top of the post. There I put wheat and breadcrumbs for the birds. I had to make my bird feeding station high enough that the horses could not reach the feed, as now they were able to get around over the many trails that they had made, and they were into everything.

Little Felix, running through the snow, seemed to think that all of this softness was on the ground for his benefit. When he fell, lying there for a few minutes, he seemed to think, "Why get up when this cushion is so heavenly under my tiny body?" Lady did not want me to handle her baby. Ruthless and frightened, she would put her ears back in protest even at my approach. The other mares seemed to love Felix as much as his mother did. They, too, objected to my going to him.

After each snowfall, from the time snow started to fly in the fall until precipitation came in the form of rain, I measured each snowfall, and by spring, we had had twenty-five feet of snow. I did not have time all winter to get lonesome. Each day was long and hard. By the time I had the animals fed and watered, it was time to lunch a little. Now wood was more of a problem than ever. All afternoon, I put in picking up what wood I could find that would burn.

For drinking water, I used melted snow, as all springs were overflowing with mucky water. Wetness was everywhere. Water oozed out of everything. The only wood that would burn (fat wood, as some people call it), was pitch.

The little chickadees were so tame that they came to me for protection. The blue jays constantly chased them.

Two weeks after the storm, snow was still very deep in many places. Only high ground had thawed out. One day, I was in preparing lunch for the animals and for myself, when Teddy started barking. I was scared stiff. I hadn't heard his voice for a long time. There had been nothing for him to bark at. Were we now having company? He barked only if someone or something was around. I dashed outside, and who did I see in the yard but the mister and missus from the ranch.

To me, they looked like two angels standing there. I was never gladder to see people. Otto had asked them by letter to come up as soon as they could get through to see how I was making out. He was afraid that I would run out of feed. He had stored two hundred pounds of wheat at their place the fall before. They brought that up just in case I needed it, but I still had feed. However, I was very happy over the little extra, just in case.

It was great to have somebody at the table with me. Though their visit was short, the sight and thought of other human beings and the sound of voices was most wonderful. They came up with a team and sled. They were on the road most of the day, coming uphill in deep snow. It was almost more than their very good team could do. They did not think the trip home would be bad, as they had a trail and would be going downhill, but they had to start back as soon as the team was rested a little. Their chores were waiting for them at home. I asked them about a possibility of Otto getting through to their place. They did not think he could make it for a while. The postman had been coming on horseback for a few days, and for many days after the storm, he was unable to get through at all. They were sure that it would be two or three weeks before Otto could get through to their place in his car. Later, when I saw them, they said that they both had been snow-blind after their trip up to see me.

Spring snows are not only hard on people, but animals suffer, too. During the winter, ranchers count the days when they may possibly have spring weather, but with spring, many times, come heartaches, because there is suffering during a spring blizzard. Little calves and lambs come into a cold world, and many perish. But people cannot but wish for spring, because after spring comes summer.

In March, I started looking for my two most beloved feathered friends, the bluebird and the robin. Not that they are friendlier or more beautiful than many of the other birds that come later, but with these two come new hope—spring, new life, babies, flowers, and food for human beings and for beast. But with all of the beauty and new hope that it brings, we must accept its cruelties and its ugliness.

Before Otto could get through, Teddy died. He was on the snow where he had tried so hard to cool his feverish head. I covered his lifeless body, and I sat in the house by a window through which I could see him in the bright moonlight, and I cried all night. The next day, I tried to dig a grave for him, but I could not see what I was doing, for hot water continually filled my eyes. I felt that, with him, I had lost all that spring stood for. When I had Teddy, I never once felt unsafe. Now I felt that I could not stay up here without him. My most wonderful friend was gone. To me, it seemed that a member of my family was gone. He'd helped to warm my heart through trying days, never asking for more than a little gratitude, which he repaid with devotion, love, and guardianship. His goodness and fidelity cut through dark days like dazzling sunlight, pouring out sympathy and affection with confidence and love.

This story was told to me by one who knew Teddy before I got him. He could not quickly grasp an order given to him by a sheepherder whose human peculiarities were confusing to him, or the herder may have been one for whom he had not worked before. Teddy was baffled; he was scolded and even shot at. I could understand his goodness and willingness for kindness. I would have gone for him as far as he would have gone for me. Life for life. I was never hurt so deeply, and I shall never forget Teddy.

Day by day, his footprints disappeared in the snow, and finally only a memory of a wonderful friend remained. After he was gone, the days for me were long and lonely, and I could not keep my mind on my work. Even Skipper was sad. He, too, had lost a wonderful friend—a friend for whom he had been willing to risk his life.

How some people can speak of a dog as a dumb brute is more than I can understand. If a dog is given a chance, there is no end to his devotion. He will stick to his master to his death. At the least sign of forgiveness for wrong, which he may not have committed, he is ready to kiss the hand that was harsh to him. If all people could have known Teddy, there would be no cruelty inflicted upon animals.

How did he know the sound of Otto's car long before I could hear the slightest sound, or when I did not even know that Otto would be up? I will never know. Teddy could always tell that Otto was coming when he was yet a mile away. When the car was pulling Teddy's Hill, he would dash up the road, and by the time Otto had made the top, Teddy was there, too. Then he rode home with Otto, and when they drove into the yard, Teddy seemed to want to say, "I tried to let you know that he was coming." When Otto walked up from the ranch, Teddy ran to meet him long before he was in sight. Now one day, Otto did come up, but Teddy was not on his special hill to meet him. Otto knew that he had come too late.

Before Otto left, we put all of the horses across the creek, as now they could do some grazing. I wanted to save what feed I had as a precaution. After this month, we still had May and June to worry about. (However, we had twelve inches of snow in August one year.)

Soon, high water would come, and the creeks, atrocious in their hurry and in their fury, would go dashing over logs that lay in their path, leaping from boulder to boulder, as if they had only minutes to reach their destination. If the horses were in their favorite pasture, they would be less apt to try to cross the creek with little Felix.

As yet, we had no bridges across any of the creeks. I had to cross on a log when I went out to see how the horses were faring. I went out almost every day, and on each such trip, I saw new flowers and birds. Each time I saw Felix, he was sweeter. The horses were now getting their fill of green grass, and all that Felix was doing was guzzling his mother's milk and playing.

My trips were not so enjoyable as they had been when I had Teddy. I missed seeing him chase after a rabbit or dispute a little pine squirrel. To his and my world, the doors had been closed by death. I was glad to go away from scenery that I had been seeing for months.

I had not noticed how many ugly scars winter had left in the yard. Packed trails that I had been walking over all winter now stood up jaggedly and dirty as snow thawed.

First on the agenda, I had to clean the yard of horse droppings that had been dropped carelessly throughout winter. Raking through new grass after all of the rubbish has been taken away, with its velvet softness and clean look, is like seeing a man freshly shaven and with a new haircut.

Now when I went to see the horses, or on a jaunt of my own, I saw many deer. These wild beauties, how they could run. I had wished many times that I could have one for a pet. I never got tired of looking at them. I followed them into the timber and dark places where the ground was carpeted with emerald-green plush softness. The air was filled with spring aroma and freshness.

I did not blame the deer for picking for their home such places of nature's loveliness. To me, walking through them was heavenly, and in them I think I would enjoy being a deer.

Otto had been up, and before he left, he said something about selecting a corral site. He had gone back in such a hurry that we really did not decide where best to put a corral. I guess I could pick a suitable place. There being a natural barrier from three sides, adjacent to the chicken house, cows would have good protection.

To build a shed, we had only to put a roof in the corner of two rock walls, which were from the west and north. Sun could come in from the east and south and should keep the cows and calves comfortable on the coldest days. Otto said that he had some milch cows spotted and thought it would be nice if I, too, saw them before closing the deal.

What I then knew about cows would have filled a nutshell, but I was willing to help, and if I had a reason for a town trip, I would not feel that I was walking out on the place now that I did not have Teddy.

The cows would be fresh soon. We would have to make a decision as quickly as possible. And Otto had located a schoolgirl who would help with the work and for my company. She would be up as soon as school was out.

We bought the cows. Tillie, a Guernsey-Jersey, and Bess, a Holstein, were both very good milch cows, and each had a nice calf, a bull and a heifer. I called them Jack and Jill.

How wonderful! Now we would have all of the milk and cream that we could use. The cows would be trucked up in a few days. My town visit was short but joyful.

This was my first trip to town in many months. When I got home, poor Skipper was gone.

The road was good now, and Otto was up several times each week. He drove up late in the evening and went back early in the morning. One day, he drove up, and as he walked across the porch, mingled with his footsteps was a little gallop. As he walked into the house, behind him walked the most quizzical little dog. His feet were much too large for him, but he looked like he would grow up to their size. I felt so bad over losing Teddy that I did not think I could ever love another dog, but when Otto told me of this little fellow's misfortune, I took him and loved him deeply.

I wanted to give him a suitable name, but I could think of none. Every time I spoke to him, I called him Teddy, so he became Teddy Number Two.

When school started, my girl went back to town, and Teddy II and I were again alone. Few people were still coming up. September, in our part of the country, is quite cold, and most people lose their enthusiasm for the mountains.

But I had to keep myself busy, so I decided that, now that we had cows, they would have to have a shed, so my job of building a shed got underway. First, I had to get the material together. I cut enough dry pine poles for the roof. Next, I got two large pitch posts, and I set them well into the ground for the southeast side of the roof to rest on. The other side of the roof would rest on the rock wall. The shed would be ten by twenty-four feet with a pole partition to separate the calves from the cows. Next, I fitted poles side by side for the roof, which I covered with a layer of dirt about eight inches thick that I threw up with a shovel; I carried the rest of the dirt up a ladder to the roof in a bucket. It kept rain and snow from the cattle, and by adding a little extra dirt once in a while, it lasted for about eight years.

On summer nights, the calves were in the yard, and the cows were in the corral. During the day, the calves were in the corral, and the cows were out. A large boulder that framed in the north side of the corral was covered with dirt on the outside almost to the top; the calves would walk up the boulder and on top of the shed roof, standing there looking down at the cows. I would almost have heart failure every time I saw them up there, but they were perfectly safe. When they were through showing off, they came down.

2

BUILDING OUR HOME TOGETHER

As time went on, Otto became my husband. We pooled our resources, and we started building our home together. For our homesite, we selected a small but pretty valley at the foot of a large mountain. It was like an oblong bowl nestled in rugged rocks and trees at an elevation of eight thousand feet and in the junction of two creeks.

We are hidden away from civilization by ridges. Our scenery all around changes from dark green, blue green, yellow green, deep pink, and lavender in the early morning sun as it creeps over a ridge to its morning hue on rocky tops that stick up out of timber-covered slopes. From the west, Bucks Peak, in its magnitude and standing like a guardian at the foot of our valley, is a landmark for many miles around. From the north, a rock wall frames in our grounds and protects us from the dreadful winter blizzards.

A formation of a rugged head of a man with waved hair tops the rock wall and looks down on our valley like a magnificent coadjutor, to which we refer as The Old Man of the Mountains. This was, no doubt, a landmark to the Indians and a symbol of friendship, for there was much evidence of them having had their workshops all through the lower ridges around our valley. In places, we found many flint chips resembling the many arrowheads that we find in this vicinity. Some are very tiny in size and were, no doubt, used for bird shots. Some are very large spearheads. There are also rock slabs which were used for utensils, and there is evidence of buffalo having been here. We can still see depressions in the earth where they wallowed.

Otto found a large buffalo skull on Elk Run Creek, which runs through our place to the east. This was one of many camping places for the Indians and their food supply. Grass, being more tender and sweet in high altitudes, and pure cool water and protection from flies drove game to the mountains from hot flats where trees are few and many miles apart and where there is only stagnant water to drink. Most all of the Indian relics have been picked up for souvenirs.

Our main creek is the east branch of Box Elder Creek, which runs through the east end of our valley. Another creek comes down from Bucks Peak and through our valley, emptying into Box Elder Creek right in our yard. This creek is not named on the map, but we have named it Meadow Creek.

Our buildings are spread out in the junction of the two creeks and on both sides. From the top of the Old Man of the Mountains, the country is visible for miles around, and our camp is right at its foot like a playhouse in a child's storybook. Our valley was covered thickly with trees and had to be cleared of much fallen timber and brush.

After we had the grounds cleared, we started clearing the valley for a hay meadow and a garden. We did not know how to go about clearing land that was so thickly covered with trees and brush. Many of the trees had grown old long before we discovered this valley, and they had fallen over in a tangled mass, and more trees had come up and had grown into a jungle.

Meadow Creek had so much brush on its banks that one could hardly cross from one side to the other. To clear this land, we thought if we cut the trees and let them lay, that in a short time, the stumps could be knocked out with little effort, and all of the rubbish could be picked up and burned at one time. And while we were waiting for the stumps to rot, we could do much building.

Fences and houses were badly needed, as in this climate and elevation, everything must be housed during the long and severe winter months. So trees were cut and left to fall where they might all the way up our valley. This job completed, we felt good, for soon we would have feed for the few head of stock that we had and that we had to board out during the winter. Now we could put in all of our time cutting building logs. So, one by one, we cut trees like two ants moving something much too large for them.

We cut, trimmed, dragged, and hauled trees, and we shaped each tree into a building log. Finally, we shaped all of the logs into many large and small buildings. The garden spot had to be cleared of sage brush and trees, for we had to grow what food we could. Much of the work had to be done as quickly as we could possibly do it, as Otto wanted to make final proof on his homestead. But while we were cutting and building and waiting, the stumps did not rot; they stayed green and sent up shoots until again our valley was a tangled mass, only now more so.

Now it was almost impossible for one to go through for all of the rubbish that lay on the ground and that grew. The stumps all had to be grubbed out.

We had to learn the hard way, never having lived under conditions like we had to cope with up here. This was all new to us, but we knew that with God's help, we could do it.

We did not let setbacks discourage us, though at times, the burden was much too heavy. We kept plodding along. We started all over to clear out the valley. Cutting and burning everything as we went along, the grass had a chance to grow, and by the time we got there, the last of the rubbish lay behind us, and there was a meadow where we could put up enough hay to feed the few head of stock that we kept. We were kept busy over many years, and we hoped that we could always be occupied, for occupation brings contentment.

When I came to live permanently in the mountains, my big problem was how much food to buy. Having lived for many years where I only had to go through an arch to a grocery store, moving to where I would be snowed in to all but horseback travel for at least six months out of the year was something to think about.

I started out by figuring how many meals we would have in the time when we could not go to the store. First on the list were the "must" things—staple groceries. Then we determined the things we most liked to eat and how many meals we would want of each of these foods. And, too, I had to have balanced meals, and so on down the line. I got along nicely. If we ran out of potatoes, we had beans, and if we did not have cream for our coffee, we drank it black.

The second year was not so hard. I made out my list as I went through the first winter, so when the time came to buy supplies the second fall, I was ready. One winter, we ran out of flour due to my not taking into consideration two cats that we had acquired, and we still had my second Teddy. By now, he had grown up to match his feet. His bread basket seemed always empty, so it took many pancakes each morning to fill us all. But we never quit eating. We had five hundred pounds of wheat that we bought for chicken feed, so in the evening, we spread some wheat on the table, and while we talked and planned, we were picking foreign substances out of the wheat, which I washed and put into the oven to dry and parch a little.

In the morning, we put the wheat through the chicken feed grinder and made it into flour. This made the best pancakes that I have ever eaten. Someday, I shall make some more.

Another problem was how to dress where the snow would be very deep during winter and the temperature would plunge without notice. We could not make the weather over to suit ourselves, so we made adjustments to suit the weather. We had to dress so that we were not too warmly dressed when indoors, but we had to put on extra clothes when we went out. That to us was just another part of our living quarters, but much larger than the house that we lived in and at times very cold, and where there is more draft and the snow sifts down one's back if not properly buttoned up. We each tried many different riggings. I settled for one type, and Otto settled for something else. We never tried to get the other one to do as we were doing. Our motto was "Each to suit his own taste."

At first, I thought that I would be warmer with more clothes, but soon I found that I was wrong. I finally settled for a suit of rayon and wool long sleeves, long leg underwear, a wool slipover sweater, jeans, heavy wool socks, sheepskin pacs, a pair of boy's four-buckle galoshes, a good wool jacket—or a leather jacket—wool-lined leather mittens, and a scotch cap. On really cold days, or in deep snow, I wear an extra pair of jeans pulled well down over the tops of my overshoes and tied around my ankles. In this rigging, on the coldest days, I am comfortable but not loaded down.

Otto dressed just about the same, only for his feet gear, he wore felt boots in his galoshes. He could not keep his feet warm in sheepskin pacs. This dress was nice for much hiking or working out in a blizzard. We worked out most all winter; for some reason, we have never ran out of work. But we did a job in love, not in hate.

Many times, we built things and then tore them down. We tore my homestead cabin down and moved the logs to our valley location, and we rebuilt the cabin for our winter quarters. We added two bedrooms, a bathroom, and a large kitchen, which made this cabin into a nice home. We also tore down a long shed that was on my place. We had put it up so that I would have proper improvements before making final proof, and which we could not use after we had established our headquarters in the valley.

We used the shed logs for a new chicken house, because the little chicken house that I had built was now too small and too near the house. Invariably, some careless person left a nice, juicy worm dangling on a hook by the house, or by a cabin, and a hen came along and ate this made-to-order tidbit and was caught on the hook in place of a fish, and I had to go out and kill the poor thing.

The corral, too, was too near the house. People came to watch us milk, and the cows held up their milk. So we selected a new chicken house and corral location up on a hill west of the other buildings. This location—like the first—is surrounded by large boulders. From here, there is a magnificent view of the mountains. Slopes covered with yellow-green lodge pole pine and blue-green spruce against a steep background of jagged rocks silhouette beautifully against the sky. Here being more isolated, the birds sang to us while we worked. The robin built her nest on shelves under the shed roof. Early in the morning as we came up to milk, their songs filled the air. Here, too, live the song sparrows, their nests in the tall lodge pole pine; they like to cradle their babies in the crown of the tall trees where they sway back and forth in the slightest breeze. The song sparrow was even friendlier than the robin; the little mother came right to us while we were milking. She hopped here and there picking up hair until she had so much in her little bill that she looked like she was wearing long whiskers. She used the hair to line her nest. When I brushed the cows, I put the hair I brushed out on the many large rocks in and around the corral where she could pick up a bill full at one time. The little pine squirrel came for the hair, too; they nested in the large ponderosa pine in and around the corral; they, too, were very friendly. During summer, the corral and shed are completely hidden away by green trees and are not visible from the main ground.

When we milked late on summer evenings, the view of the mountains was beautiful in a full, brilliant moon, gleaming and throwing shadows. And from a distance out of the rugged ridges came the song of a lone coyote, pouring out his love to his mate. It made one appreciate nature's enchanting beauty in a moon-filled night.

Suddenly, one feels rested after a long and hard day and not in a hurry to go into the house, but rather slowly going the long way around so as to see more of a heavenly night.

Otto built a nice house on his homestead where friends could stay over on weekends. Soon, friends brought friends, and our two places became a large playground. We found ourselves in the recreation business.

Our place is now known as the Silver Spruce Lodge.

As soon as we were established, some of the Congregational ministers made arrangements for a summer camp for their young people at our place. They had about seventy-five people, but we did not have housing for that many.

This problem was solved by getting a large tent, sixteen by thirty-five feet, where food was prepared and served. The assembly brought two large tents for sleeping quarters. With this arrangement, everybody was housed nicely. The place looked like a circus ground, but it was real camp life for the young people, and they all seemed to enjoy it.

Their program consisted of religious training in the forenoon, with recreation in the afternoon and a campfire in the evening. During morning classes, most anyplace one looked, there were young people in a circle with an instructor in their midst—under trees, on the creek bank, on the lodge porch, and just anyplace on the green grass.

The instructor stayed at the same post, but at the end of a given time, his group went to another post, and a group from one of the other posts came to his post. In this way, all of the young people benefitted from all of the teachers, some of which were foreign missionaries.

Each group living together was known by a name they chose. Each morning, living quarters were inspected by a special group. The inspection committee consisted of some of the older people.

Their paper was the "Scandal Sheet," and it was read after the evening meal. All reports were made by this paper—good or bad—concerning minister or pupil, cook or president; all got the same treatment. This paper had the best news hounds in the country.

For Sunday morning services, the young people selected a place under the large ponderosa pine, with a rock background and a lovely front view of the rugged terrain. To the east, Castle Rock daringly stood convincingly of a Divine Power. To the south, there are high jagged ridges, black and green. Kettle Mountain, against a heavenly blue sky and bathed in the hot sun, stands like a crazy house in a fairy-tale book. Standing watch by day and by night over God's creatures, offering protection in the many gaping holes in her sides, she majestically accepts the wilderness around her. Its roughness, its rigorousness, its beauties, and new life unchangingly stand from century to century.

The mighty ponderosa pine, with its huge arm-like branches outstretched, seems to say, "Come, all ye faithful. I will protect you while you worship your God." And to make the setting still more beautiful, Mother Nature sprinkled the surroundings with her lively flowers.

Many visitors came to these services, and if the weather was nice, they stayed to enjoy the rest of the day. While the older people visited with friends in camp, the youngsters were out climbing mountains or were on top of the Old Man of the Mountains, while some took a dip in the creek.

When the time came for camp to break up, there were many sad faces. Parting with friends that were made over a week at camp was hard. I am sure that each young person took home a beautiful memory and a spiritual benefit. Some of the young people grew up while coming to this camp and have married, and now their children come. Over twenty successive years, much has happened, but this group has never missed coming up. They now number well over a hundred people.

Our place and the assembly grew up together like two infants. We looked forward to their coming like we looked for our own kinsfolk, and since it was very hard for both Otto and I to go away at one time, which was necessary once in a while, we took advantage of a good opportunity, and we turned the place over to the assembly while we went to town for the day to take care of important business or to shop for things that we liked to select together. There was only one thing that we were not able to talk them into doing—milking the cows.

At the birth of the assembly, another group was looking for a place where they could relax and rest for a few days with plenty of good food to eat and a good place to sleep. They came to look our place over. Oh, it would do—no telephone and not much road; surely no one could find them up here. They were all businessmen who wanted to forget shop for a few days. The next year, they came again, and the bunch was larger. Now, after twenty-four successive years, this group fills our place to capacity. They have had many good laughs while coming to our place, and they have hiked over many miles of beautiful trails along the streams and over hills. And I have cooked and served many meals to them, which they always seemed to enjoy.

I remember one year when they were at our place. I was busy in the kitchen preparing another meal for them when I heard much laughter in the yard. I did not have time to see what funny game they might be playing this time, but I did just happen to look out of the back door in time to see my ducks going to the creek the long way around and singing what I took to be "Show me the way to go to the creek." They were falling over everything they came to.

First in line was the drake, and then there was the mama duck, and finally there were all of the little ducklings, all cutting antics as they went along. When they got to the creek, they did not slide into the water gracefully like a duck does. They just fell in. I could not comprehend what had happened to my poor ducks; they were acting so queer. I thought that they must have eaten something that poisoned them. I wanted to do something for them, but I did not know what I could do; they seemed so very sick.

I thought, "There is no use. They will all be dead in a few minutes." I just stood in the door and watched them. They started drinking water as soon as they got to the creek. They just could not seem to quench their thirst. They just kept drinking, and finally they'd had enough. They put their heads under their wings and floated on the water. I went back to my job of cooking, thinking that it must be the way a duck dies of poisoning. After what seemed like an hour, I went out to look at them. They were still floating on the water like they were dead.

I called to them. The drake looked up at me and blinked his eyes and said something to another duck. They both stood up in the water and flapped their wings and squawked like they were having a big laugh over the whole thing. Yes, it is true. Those ornery big boys put some corn in a pan and poured whiskey over it and fed it to my ducks. How near they came to having stewed duck for dinner they will never know.

Another time, they were having a calf-riding contest. This time, I looked out of the window just in time to see a man lying on the ground, a calf hightailing it into the timber and another man riding after it on a stick horse. Oh, yes, in this bunch, there are some very good actors. How these men escaped Hollywood may someday be revealed. Oh, well, boys will be boys.

They did not officially take a name for their group, so we called them the Sprucesters. What their wives call them may never be revealed.

Developing a playground was a lot of fun. The job I enjoyed most was taking people on hiking trips. Otto and I have taken the assembly youngsters to the top of Bucks Peak many times, and if Otto was busy, I went with the help of one of the ministers. I took the lead, and the minister brought up the rear. Going up in that manner, we could keep the youngsters together.

There is no trail up this mountain. We just stumbled our way up and down, but the trip was worth all of the skinned shins and ripped clothes. The elevation must be around ten thousand feet. Standing on top, facing east and looking directly down through treetops, we saw jagged hogback ridges and canyons. Down at the foot, we saw our valley. Through field glasses, we could plainly see buildings, parked cars, and people walking around in the yard. As we lifted our eyes on and on, we saw jagged mountains.

In a haze, about fifty miles as the crow flies, standing in its glory, tall and pointed, is Laramie Peak. For centuries, a God and early Indian and white trapper, a mark of distance to the early stage coachran, bullwhacker and mule skinner. To the tourist of today, it is a reminder of a hard and adventurous past within its boundaries, and it is a landmark for many, many miles around. Through all of the years, it has stood head high, an unending helper to all travelers.

Looking at any level, as we turned, we saw mountains—rounded, jagged, near, far, very high, less high, flat topped, and pointed. About seven miles to the north, we saw buildings on the U.S. grant ranch, and farther yet in the background, we saw more beautiful mountains, deep green, streaked with yellow green, deep lavender, indigo, and purple black. Thirty miles down, we saw smoke curling up to the sky from the oil refinery in Glenrock. In a great distance like a picture hanging from the sky are the mighty Big Horn Mountains. About forty miles to the west, we saw Casper Mountain, and in its foothills, we saw smog from the many refineries and much industry in and around Casper.

All around us were more mountains, one after another. To the south at Bucks Peak, sticking up like an ice cream cone, is Twin Peak, seemingly so near that we could step to its top. Between Duck and Twin Peaks is a canyon leading to the east branch of Box Elder Creek. We saw the creek through treetops gleaming in a bright sun like a jewel on the floor of another canyon, curling, twisting like a silver worm, swiftly running on and on through the east end of our valley and eventually at the ranch below, emptying into the main part of Box Elder Creek. Then, between Glenrock and Douglas, the main branch of Box Elder empties into the North Platte River to contribute its share to the mighty flow of rushing waters from Cortes, Pathfinder, and

Alcova dams, pouring out over much of Wyoming and into Nebraska to bring parched lands into paradise valleys.

To the south stands Kettle Mountain, comparatively as high as Bucks Peak, but much more defying when climbing to its top. Here and there we saw, peeking in between mountaintops, the Laramie Plains. Over all the land, in valleys and on mountaintops, is the loveliness of flower-covered meadows scattered like colorful crazy quilt patches dropped here and there by a careless hand.

While one group of mountain climbers went to Bucks Peak, I took the less capable youngsters to Mount Julie; this mountain got its name from the young people, because I was first to take them to the top. This climb is not as hard as Bucks Peak, and it is not as far to the top. Being on the southwest side as we went up, ridges and tree-covered slopes seemed to crouch, squat, and finally flatten before our eyes and were beautifully visible all the way as we went up and up. Elk Run Creek, glowing here and there through treetops, empties into our east branch of Box Elder Creek, which we could follow with our eyes from our camp to the junction of Elk Run Creek and down until finally we lost sight of it.

Before we reached the top of Mount Julie, we went through a small canyon, coming from the top of this mountain. To me, this is the most wonderful part of the trip. The canyon itself is beautiful, and the scenery as we looked down was out of this world. We saw our camp, the two creeks, and Bucks Peak and many more mountains and ridges. As far as our eyes could see, there was beauty. One never sees the same thing in the same light. Before we reached the top of Mount Julie, mountains started to stick up to the north, one ridge and then another that we could see at such close range from this spot only, throwing shadows and colors into small canyons. Gold spots appeared here and there as the sun came through to show more beauty.

Our valley, from this mountaintop, was most beautiful, because we could see it without the aid of field glasses. We could plainly see people walking in the yard. It all seemed like a big picture and not a reality. Coming down, we were on the southeast side of this mountain. We went through huge boulders with gorgeous ponderosa pine crowding against the rocks. Some seemed to be growing out of the rocks with only a crevasse to support their huge roots.

At one place, we sat down and slid through a deep, narrow shoot between rock walls to reach the next landing. Finally, we were down in a lovely lodge pole pine forest still sprinkled with the huge and mighty ponderosa. We cut up into lumber some of the many large pine trees that grew on our place. For the first few buildings that we had put up on our homesteads, we had lumber trucked up from Glenrock, which made it very expensive, so we decided to get a lumber mill and cut our trees into lumber.

Otto's old Hupmobile finally conked out, so he used the engine for power to run the lumber mill. When he put it into high gear, we sliced boards from huge logs like slicing bread from a loaf. As soon as the sawmill got into operation, I found use for all of the by-products. The clean sawdust was my big weakness. Some I used for cow bedding, and we packed ice in it, too. I enjoyed lying on it in the hot sun, smelling the sweet odor of freshly cut pine. It was fun being around the sawmill and watching it work. Machinery does things so graciously. It was all so exciting to be on the job and not be working. But my freedom was short. I am usually like a loose end flopping around—the first thing I know, I am tied down to something. But I guess I like it this way, or I would not be hanging around.

In this case, I was tied down to the job of taking the boards away as they were being cut and stacking them into very neat stacks, each according to length and layers so that air could circulate through and dry the lumber out. In no time, Otto and I were operating the sawmill like two veterans—he being the sawyer and I the take-off woman.

Our buildings scattered on both sides of the creek junction are connected by many bridges. The first building constructed on Otto's place was the lodge, which is thirty-five by fifty feet. It has three bedrooms, a large living and recreation room with a rugged rock fireplace built into the room, and a large kitchen. The kitchen is one of the principle places of interest, and it is where people spent much time visiting while I prepared food for them, which was served in the living room. There are three cabins, twelve by twenty feet, completely equipped for housekeeping. A cookhouse was put up for large groups; it has a large dining room, kitchen, and a bedroom for the cooks. This building rests right on the bank of Box Elder Creek and is twenty-six by fifty feet. This is the first building that Otto and I put up together. The assembly kitchen staff seemed to have the best time of all.

Hoisting Flag On Mount Julie

Mrs. Deejten, the head chef, Mrs. Castlow the kingfish, and many of the cook maids all lived together in the cookhouse bedroom. They enjoyed preparing and serving food to the many young people and their leaders. Of all people in camp, they got the most compliments, not only for their delicious food, but because they were a bunch of real angels, flying around always on time and never anyone flying out of the many openings this summer building has. When Mrs. Deejten started concocting her hors d'oeuvres, all of the animals that lived with us were in danger, but it always tasted and smelled heavenly.

The second building we put up is the winter barn. This building is in a beautiful setting, a place where I always wanted to build my home, on a hill and against a mountain for protection from deep snow. This building is thirty-five by fifty feet. The view from here is beautiful, looking into our valley.

When the weather was very cold, the cows watched us as we started from the house, and they began lining up in the barn. The lead cow stood in the doorway, which was just an opening, and not one of the other dumb brutes tried to go by until she was ready to start. When she knew that we were almost to the haystack, which was in trees for protection, she came out, and all the other stock had to follow in their turn. Our stock traveled in a line, each in its proper turn, and none could take another's place unless it first fought another one out of line. Lady lived with the cows, but as a rule, she came down to the valley to walk to the haystack with us.

Our third building is the Goons Grotto, and it is thirty-six by sixty feet with two stories; it is nestled in a pine forest and on a rocky knoll. In it are three hundred logs; this was a big undertaking. After the walls were too high for us to lift the logs, we used pulleys, and for this job, Otto had some irons made to drive into the logs. We called them iron-men; they helped hold the log being lifted up. The icehouse was place to put up its twelve by twelve feet with a dirt roof. Here we packed ice for summer cooking. We got our ice from a large beaver dam. At one time, the ice dam was so near the icehouse that all we had to do was slide the ice over a few boards into the house. It washed out, and we had to go farther upcreek for ice.

As a rule, we had to clear the snow from the creek where we cut ice so that the ice would freeze thick enough for packing. Since snow acts like an insulator, it keeps the ice from forming. While we waited for the ice to get thick enough for packing, we used the lake for ice skating. Raised in Wisconsin, Otto was a good ice-skater; coming from Texas, I am no ice-skater at all.

When we first started skating, I got a busted fanny the first thing, but I thought, busted or no busted, I would learn to ice-skate. I could roller-skate when I was a kid, so it should not have been too difficult. After the first week of ice skating, I could stand up on my feet with my ice skates on, but only because it hurt to sit down.

In putting up ice, we worked together like we did on all other jobs. While I cut, Otto fished the cakes out of the water, trimmed them, and dragged them up on the bank. When all of the ice was cut, Otto hauled it in on a horse-drawn sled, and I worked in the icehouse, placing the cakes and packing them. The cakes were placed twelve inches from the wall and one inch apart; between the cakes, snow was firmly packed. Between the wall and the ice, sawdust was packed, and the top was also covered with sawdust. When the ice was all packed, it was one large cake frozen together. The cakes were cut twelve by sixteen inches; we packed thirty cakes in a layer, and there were four layers. This much ice lasted all summer.

We booked another group of young people for summer camp—about thirty-five Catholic youngsters from the eastern part of the state. We arrange the place to suit each group. Now we had housing enough; one of the cabins was used for a chapel where morning and evening services were held. Later, the chapel was moved to the Grotto. The other two cabins were occupied by boys with a priest in each cabin for a chaperone. The girls used the lodge and cottage for their living quarters. We have also had the Girl Scouts and 4-H boys. Before we had housing enough, many times Otto and I took a bedroll and slept under the stars.

3

ANIMALITY

I especially enjoyed taking little people on hiking trips. With those who could not keep up with the big folks, I played a game. As we went through the woods, we each took the name of an animal that lived in our part of the country. When we got tired, we sat down to rest. Each one ululated like the animal that he represented. Sometimes a cow barked and a dog mewed, but I pretended to know all of the ululations.

Okay, we have a coyote. I tell them all about a coyote. He is our enemy, because he eats our chickens, turkeys, and baby deer. Sometimes he catches a little calf and kills it. However, he does not always eat what he kills. He kills because he is a killer by nature. For this reason, we must try to destroy him, so we hunt and trap him at every opportunity. He is very hard to trap. He is suspicious and very cautious. He can detect a trap that had been set with utmost care.

After the first story, the youngsters tired more easily, because they wanted to hear another story, so we picked another nice spot by the creek. I counted noses and checked that all of my gadabouts were all right, and I told them about another animal. What do we have now? Oh, a lynx cat. They are beautiful animals with a yellowish-gray coat of soft fur all over their bodies with only the exception of the belly, which is black and white spotted and where the fur is much longer and softer. They prowl at night like most wild animals. Their eating habits are like those of a coyote, and they are almost as bold. They are not afraid to come right into our yard and sniff at bones that the dog has been chewing. Our house cats are deathly afraid of them. We have a mother cat that a man at a roadside filling station gave us. Some tourists had taken it on a trip, and when they got out at the filling station, they also let the cat out, but what they did not take into consideration was the many buildings that it could and would go under, and it would not come out when called. Cats are not as enthusiastic about trips as dogs are.

After trying for hours to get it out from under a building, they had to go on without it. Later, I became the owner. I named her Chickum. When she saw the big out of doors, she did not know what to do. She was afraid to go out alone. If I went with her, she had a good time, but when I came into the house, so did she. Finally, when she was acquainted with the place, she had a wonderful time climbing the trees, and later yet, she discovered that there were mice and gophers in little holes in the ground. She learned to catch them, and she went hunting at night with our two other cats.

She would not eat mice or gophers but would bring them to me. But I did not eat them, either, but I gave her food that she liked in exchange for her game. One day, I came home from the garden, and she let me in the yard; she was benevolent and ran to the porch where she had three gophers in a pile. She was trying to show me that while I worked in the garden, she was by no means idle, and I owed her many things for her catch. In a case of this kind, she got a can of sardines or some canned chicken. She really enjoyed this food. After about three years with us, she had one kitten. This being a male kitten, our Tommy wanted to do away with it.

Poor Chickum was continually in hot water. One night, she brought her baby to my bed and laid it on my arm; I woke frightened, thinking that she had brought me a live mouse. I brushed her poor baby off on the floor. As it fell, I heard a tiny cry, and I quickly picked it up. I told Chickum how sorry I was. I understood what she wanted of me. She had to go outside and was afraid to leave her baby for fear that Tommy would get it while she was away. The next day, I made a little house for her and her baby; the only opening was a round hole in one end just large enough for Chickum to go through. I made a bed in the house and put her baby in it. She was so happy, because she could sit in the door, and Tommy could not get her baby. After the kitten had his eyes open, he played with his mother's tail as she sat in the little door. Finally, Tommy played with the kitten, too, and I named him Skeezix.

One night, Chickum brought me a mouse; she, no doubt, was hungry, and she thought night was as good a time to trade me a mouse for food that was cooked as day would be. But I was asleep, and I did not know that she had put a mouse on my pillow until I awakened the next morning. I felt something so nice and soft against my cheek as my head lay on the pillow. I thought, "What the heck? My pillow is not this soft." When I looked, there was a nice fat mouse that I had, no doubt, slept on most of the night. This was one morning I really felt mousy, but after a good facial and a hair wash, I did not feel mousy anymore. For all that I know, the mouse may have been alive when Chickum put it on my pillow; it ran into my hair, and I put my big noggin on it. But it did not bother me. I did not know that I was sleeping with my head on a mouse. I sleep like I work—hard. No sleeping pills or night cap are needed.

"Bow-wow! Woof!" That could be our Rex. I get great pleasure from my relationship with animals—dogs, cows, cats, horses, and some of the less ferocious wild animals. But now, I must settle down to talk about one of my best friends, the dog.

Dogs are always playing an important part in the lives of us self-styled, higher animals. I could cover page after page talking about dogs, but to some people, this would be monotonous.

When Rex was still very young, I taught him to bring me his pan when I wanted to feed him. Now, he has so completely connected his pan with food that as soon as I get up from the table, he runs to get his pan. When he has finished eating what I gave him, he picks his pan up, holding it in his mouth, and he sits up rolling his eyes, pleading for a little dessert. He always gets a tidbit of some kind. When the members of the assembly are out here, he sometimes takes his pan to the cookhouse where the young people eat; when he sits up holding his pan in his comical way and starts to roll his eyes, no one can deny him food.

Last year when the Sprucesters were up, he saw a lot of activity in the living room; he went in there with his pan, and when he came back into the kitchen, he plunked the pan on the floor behind me. I heard a rattle in it, and I looked back to see what he had brought in. He had fifty-five cents in his pan that he had collected in the living room. He seemed so put out that the money was not food that he just stood looking at it.

The cutest thing yet was one day when I was sitting on a rock cleaning fish by the little creek that flows right by the house. Otto was in the house, and Rex was sitting by me, watching me work. I had to have a pan for my clean fish. I called to Otto, "I need a pan." Before Otto had time to come out with a pan, I felt a nudge on my back and heard a little growl; that's how Rex talks to us. I looked back, and Rex was standing behind me holding his pan in his mouth and wiggling his little body all over, trying to get me to hurry to take his pan before Otto could come out with his pan. I took the pan and told him how nice he was to bring it to me, and I used it for the fish trimmings. He seemed so happy, and when Otto came out, Rex ran to meet him and tried in his way to tell Otto that he had brought me a pan and he, Otto, could take his pan back into the house, for we did not need it. I sat there laughing so hard at Rex, not paying attention to my job, and when I looked down, my fish were being washed down the creek. I had to hurriedly slide from the bank into the water to puddle my fish. Rex was so very happy to have performed a helpful deed.

He loves to go with us when we take people on hiking trips, and he dearly loves little children. Very often, he takes it upon himself to guard a little child that has gone out on a trek of its own. We can always find the wanderer by calling Rex.

He sleeps in his house, and first thing in the morning, we let him into the house, and we make a fuss over him. He enjoys it so much that he sits up and tries to laugh with us; he wrinkles his nose and shows his teeth—that's how he laughs. His expression is so quizzical that he makes us laugh the harder.

When we go to town, he has to stay at home, and that is when his spirit is really doused. If we come home before dark, he is sitting on a hill about three miles down the road, waiting for us, to get a ride home. But if we are late coming home, we usually see two sets of tracks—one going down, and the other one coming up. He had been down on his hill, but the wait was too long.

The emotion that an animal like Rex feels is more than some people can understand. We live with our animals, and they live with and for us. We understand them, and they understand us.

In the morning, we go out to the corral, and we speak a good morning to the cows or the horse. In reply, we get a good morning in their way from them. Lady makes a sound in her throat like she is laughing. "Ha, ha, ha!" And Fredrica, the cow, has a way of greeting us by sticking her tongue out as far as she can, and she says a low, "Moo." If we are passing near our cows in the pasture, they always expect a hug around the neck or a pat on the face. After they have had a bit of affection, they start to graze again, but if we go by, not paying them a little visit, they stand looking at us after we have long passed them. I guess, at a time like this, they wonder why we did not stop. They expect a little fellow feeling in return for their friendliness.

Rex has been punished only once, and then he was not to blame, but he had to learn that he was doing something that was forbidden him. After a busy summer, he had to have a little training in obedience. Having so many youngsters to play with, he sometimes forgets to mind. Our two other dogs were wonderful, too.

My first Teddy was almost human. When he died, I said that I never wanted another dog. The heartache is too great when giving up an animal that has been faithful and devoted for many years. Two different times, we were without a dog only a short time, but we soon found out that, living in the wilderness, one must have a dog. In no time after each Teddy left us, the wild creatures moved in. Skunks lived under the house. That was not too bad—they are good mousers—but when they had a discrepancy among themselves, it was just too bad. Our house cats were afraid to go out, because the lynx cats were in the yard waiting for them; they hunt house cats to kill them. And the coyote sang to us from a nearby boulder.

As soon as people found out that we had lost our first Teddy, offers of a dog came from many. In one of the oil fields, someone dropped a puppy. Youngsters took him home, but they were not allowed to keep him. His feet were too big—he would grow up to be a big dog, and it would take too much food to keep him—so, brokenhearted, the youngsters had to take him away and again drop him. This happened over many times until one of the oil field men picked him up and took him to Otto to take up to our mountains. (Otto was still working in town at the time.) In his predicament, we were glad to give him a home; he proved to be most deserving. He did grow up to match his feet; he was a mixture of collie and shepherd. He also loved people; each summer, he seemed to look forward to the assembly coming, and I am sure he knew that we were preparing for their coming. When the first truckload rolled in, he was there to greet everybody. After camp, as the young people started getting ready to go home, Teddy was posing for pictures; he got a hug from them all before they started climbing into the truck for their return trip. He performed many good deeds that we knew nothing about and many that we did know about and that we will always remember.

I always think how terrible it must be for a little animal to be taken away from home and be dropped. Country people take them to town, and town people take them to the country and leave them to find a home or to be killed—or, worse yet, to starve to death. It is so much more humane to do away with an animal in a way that it does not have to suffer if we cannot keep it.

When we both went to town, Teddy watched the place. He had learned that when chickens started running and squawking, something was after them. He did not give a hawk a chance to swoop down to pick up a chicken; many times, he had a hawk treed by the time I got out with my twelve-gauge, double-barreled shotgun that kicked like a bad mule. When I got ready to fire the old thing, I first had to hug a nearby tree and then press the old cannon to my shoulder and pull the trigger; then I would spin for a while before I once more got my balance. By the time I was over the shock, I never knew if I had killed what I'd shot at had it not been for Teddy standing by the kill. Teddy lived with us to a ripe old age of twelve and a half years. We were very sad when he left us, but we knew that he had served his time on earth and that now he had earned his rest in a peaceful sleep. I buried him by my first Teddy.

And what do we have now? Oh, this is good. This youngster does not how his animal speaks, so he is trying to act it out; since we have no kangaroo, he must be a deer.

1946 was a wet spring. On June 12, 1946, Otto had to go on horseback after the mail due to much snow. After coming home from the pasture with his saddle horse, he said that he'd run across tiny fawn tracks; there seemed to be only the fawn and no mother. Did I want to go see about this little fawn? He described the location to me, and I had no trouble finding the tracks. They were in many places. After walking around a little, I found the tiny fawn under a sage brush. I sat down by it and stroked it with my hand. Its body was as soft as velvet. I had never seen anything so sweet. I put it in my lap and loved it. Those tiny feet and big eyes! I picked it up and started home with it. I had walked only a few feet when I saw another one under another sage brush. I picked it up, too. It was hurt. There was a deep scratch across its face and a hole through one ear like some animal had mauled it. I went home with one under each arm.

I called them Topsy and Wopsy. Topsy's spots were helter-skelter, whereas Wopsy's were in a line. We had a bunch of bum lambs that spring, so feeding the fawns was no problem. I had bottles and nipples, but I did not know how much milk they should have at a feeding. Since Otto was going down after the mail, I asked him to find out how much milk I should give a fawn at a feeding. I was sure down the line someone would know. I was told, "Start them the same as a lamb—a third of a cup of warm milk to a feeding, four times a day."

At first, they would not take the bottle, but as soon as they found out it was milk, they went to work.

Topsy and Wopsy in the Wading in the Creek

The milk disappeared quickly, and they squealed for more. Their cries were like that of a little kitten.

Topsy got along nicely, but Wopsy was sick. He quit eating. I was afraid that I would lose him. I got all of the information I could from the neighbors on how to care for him. I went to see a veterinarian. He told me what to do. And still milk did not agree with him. Wopsy did not want much of anything to eat. I boiled his milk, and I tried canned milk. Finally, I tried Pablum and cod liver oil. I fed him out of a spoon like a baby. One day, he decided that he liked Pablum and cod liver oil and started to eat, and he was ready for his bottle, too. Little by little, he improved. He began going out with Topsy. He kept going through the grass looking for something. Finally, he found what he wanted—a form of milkweed.

Each day, he went to this same weed and nibbled a little of it. Nature told him that this would make him well. Little sympathetic Topsy gave him all the possible encouragement. She seemed to tell him to eat, and lie in the sun, and wet places and to eat mud, while she like a guardian angel, devotedly stood by to make sure that nothing disturbed him. He ate mud by the mouthful, and he lay in it; it probably cooled his feverish body. As he got stronger, it was she who found good concealment for him where he could rest undisturbed, never once going more than a few feet from him. If I found her hideout, she immediately found a new place in rocks or in the woods where she would conceal Wopsy until it was almost impossible to see him. As soon as I caught on to her tricks, I kept check on her without letting her know that I knew about her hideaway. Finally, Wopsy recovered completely, and they became the sweetest pets that I have ever had. I shall always remember their little patent leather noses and soft bodies. Everyone who knew them loved them. Now they were always ready to eat at feeding time.

All I had to do was click the bottles together, and if they were within hearing distance, they came on a run. They and the lambs were like a bunch of rowdy youngsters. They frolicked all over the place. The one thing they enjoyed most was racing across the front porch, around the house, and over the porch again. This always happened when some of the guests were taking a nap, and I was trying to be very quiet. Many times, the hubbub began so suddenly that I thought it was thundering. The lambs and deer always seemed to try to outdo one another. They would get up on a rock and nibble on tender tree branches that they had to stretch their little necks to reach. They would stand on the very edge of a big rock, standing on tiptoes, to reach the branches farthest away. While I stood watching and holding my breath, I expected them to come sliding down any minute, but they never did. They stood there as though glued to the rocks, bending this way and that way as if unjointed, and all of a sudden, one would jump from a rock, and here they would all come kicking up their heels, twisting their bodies like a bunch of fancy dancers.

Since they were not penned up, we had to remember to check on them now and then so they would not take a notion to keep going once they were started. If the place was unusually quiet, the first place we looked for them was in the clover patch in the meadow. On hot days, we usually found them in the chicken house, bedded down in the straw fast asleep. In order to get into the chicken house, they had to go up six steps, but that seemed to be an inducement. Through August and into September, Topsy and Wopsy lost their spots and began to take on the look of real deer, and they were more alert.

With their spots, they lost their feeling of security, but they grew more beautiful by the day. On wash days, they were attracted by the clothes on the line. Wopsy walked on his hind legs under the clothesline and would strike at the clothes with his front feet, and I went after him with a stick. Then he would buck and dance all around me and seemed to say, "Let's see who can butt harder." I had no desire to teach him to use his antlers. Now they were only buttons and probably a little itchy, but someday, he would know how to protect himself with them. I did not want to make a fighter out of him. He had an ugly enough disposition as it was.

He did not like dogs or cats. Rex was a tiny puppy, and both Topsy and Wopsy tried to kill out in the yard. How he escaped from being badly hurt when they jumped on him with all four hoofs is more than I know. He was slightly hurt one time after he stuck his head from under the porch and surveyed the territory before coming out. I was in a constant dilemma. The deer chewed up everything within their reach. Topsy was especially fond of a pink nightie. If I hung it on the line by the top, she chewed a little from the bottom, and if I hung it by the bottom, she chewed the top. On wash days, she went around looking for this particular garment. Finally, the nightie came to my knee on one side and dragged the floor on the other side and the top took on a lacy look, so I put it away as a remembrance to Topsy.

When they were little, they stayed in the house much of the time. Their favorite bed was the couch in the living room. They jumped up and curled their little bodies around the cushions like two kittens. They seemed to enjoy the softness under their bodies. There they would sleep for hours. When I heard a thump on the floor, I knew that they had jumped from the couch, and if I did not put them out, I might have puddle on the floor or some little marbles rolling around. I housebroke them by putting them outside as soon as they got up from a nap. In no time, they went to the door and cried. Finally, they went to the door and pushed, and they learned to open the screen door.

As they grew older and the weather was warmer, they stayed out of doors all the time. When we came home from town, they were on hand to see what we brought home. If we left the car door open, they went right in and immediately went to work eating anything they could get to. They loved apples, watermelon, candy, cookies, raisins, crackers, and cigarettes. They were always looking for cigarette butts, and somebody taught them to drink something out of a bottle other than milk. I think I could put my finger on the guilty parties.

One day, when we came home from town, Topsy and Wopsy came into the house with me. I took my hat off and put it on the bed, and in no more time than I could blink my eye, Topsy had my hat, and before I could grab it, she had the veil in her mouth, chewing as hard as she could, and when I got the hat away from her, the veil was gone. How she could put so much into her mouth so quickly was something only she could answer. That sweet little mouth of hers did not miss a thing.

Many times, I had to force their mouths open to get something out that they should not have had. I was always on needles and pins for fear that they would get something of value that some of the guests left around. One day, a lady started to put on a silk shirt, and the collar was completely chewed up. I felt bad about this, but she seemed to think that she had something to take home to show her friends—a deer-chewed shirt. But with all of their faults, we all loved them.

That fall, when the Sprucesters were up, they had target practice. As soon as Topsy and Wopsy heard shooting, they came to the back door and wanted in. I figured that they were frightened by the gunshots, so I let them in. They went to our bedroom, and Topsy jumped up on the bed and curled into a ball and went to sleep. Wopsy lay by the bed on a rug, and he slept, too. They knew that in the house they were safe.

We could always tell when a storm was brewing. Topsy and Wopsy would put on a show. They stood on their hind legs and boxed with their front feet like two people boxing, and all of a sudden, they would take out across the meadow, running so fast that they seemed only a streak dashing through the air. This was their way of having fun. After a good frolic, they came to me for a little petting.

After much running, they panted with their mouths open and their sides going in and out like an accordion. If I could have had a movie camera, I could have taken some wonderful pictures of their many performances. I could never sneak away from them. They always seemed to know if I wanted to go someplace without them. Sometimes I ran away and tried to hide in the rocks, and I would get up on a high point to watch them. I would be gone only a few minutes, and they would start to trail me like a dog, their noses to the ground. The hotter my trail got, the faster they came. They always seemed to be happy when they found me.

They would aggravate me most when I went fishing. The very pool I wanted to fish in, they wanted to wade in, and there was no way of keeping them out. One day, Otto went upcreek for a stroll, and the deer went with him. When they were well on their way, I decided that this would be my chance to go fishing alone. I went to Elk Run Creek so that I would be sure not run into those pests. They and Otto went up Box Elder Creek. The two creeks are about one mile apart. I had just gotten to Elk Run Creek when I heard something behind me. I looked back, and who was there but Topsy! Her little mouth was open wide, and her sides were puffing out. She had run so hard to catch up with me. I was mad at her, but I put my arms around her neck and told her, "We girls must stick together." She seemed so happy when I loved her. No doubt, she expected a spanking. I was worried about Wopsy not being with her, as I had never known of them being separated. How Topsy knew I went to the other creek I did not know, since each creek is in a different direction.

Topsy and Wopsy Resting on the Cottage Porch

Otto said that Topsy had slipped away, and he did not know that she followed me. He thought she went exploring on her own.

Wopsy did not see her leave, and when he had discovered that she was not there, Otto said that he simply went wild. Otto called him and talked to him, and finally he settled down. I gave up fishing, and instead, Topsy and I had a long hike. As we were going up a valley along a creek with mountians on both sides, I heard a peculiar voice coming from the top of one of the mountains. Topsy heard it, too. It was a love call that she understood. She answered it, and immediately I saw something move behind a big rock, and it started down the mountainside. She ran up to meet it. I thought, "Here is where I lose Topsy." A big buck was coming to her.

She looked him over and started back to me as unconcerned as you please. I stood perfectly still. Topsy came to me, and I rubbed her face. The buck came almost to me and stood looking at me. He was a beautiful animal. His antlers stood on his head like a branched tree. Topsy seemed to say to him, "Go away. I am only a little girl out to see what is on this side of a mountain that I have never been over before, and on my first trip away from home, I find a vagabond lover!" He wanted Topsy to follow him. He kept coaxing and coming closer to me. Topsy stood by my side, hardly moving. I was afraid. Never had I been so near one of those big fellows.

I have heard that a buck will attack a person. He made no attempt to go away until I spoke and moved toward him. Then he bounced. I was relieved when that gorgeous creature was gone, and I was happy that Topsy did not go away with him. She, no doubt, remembered that I told her, "We girls must stick together."

Fall came, and I started to trap. Then my troubles really started. Every morning, I was always afraid that they would get their feet into a trap. They always went over my trapline with me. They seemed to want to know why I had bait hanging on a tree and why they could not go to it. If I had an animal in a trap, their backs raised as stiffly as big bristles, and they hit the ground with their feet. I always killed my catch as quickly as possible so as to avoid trouble. By now, the deer had made up with Rex, as he, too, was running the trapline with me. The three played continually as we went along. I had much fun watching them play.

On our way home, we came by a haystack. There Topsy and Wopsy stopped to feed and to sleep in the soft hay. They would stand by the haystack, and as if they had wings, they jumped to the top, and then they would paw the hay and go around for a while. When their bed was to their liking, they lay down and went to sleep, and then they came to the house where they would lay on the porch to chew their cud. They enjoyed sleeping in the snow if there was no wind.

One morning, after an all-night snow, I was worried about them. The snow was about three feet deep. I could see no sign of them anyplace. Every few minutes, I walked to the window to see if I could see any sign of them. As I stood before the window, before my eyes, something popped out of the snow. It looked like a rabbit and another one and two more. I thought, "Gee-gosh, where are all of the rabbits coming from all of a sudden?" I had not seen a rabbit for some time. The snow started to lift up, and out came Topsy and Wopsy. They lay there and let the snow cover them completely. The rabbit-like things were their ears. As they moved their heads, an ear stuck up out of the snow, appearing suddenly, until it looked like four rabbits sat on top of the snow.

I had made a windbreak on the porch and put some hay there for a bed for them. During a blizzard, they slept there. When they ate up their bed, Otto brought them more hay. One night, the temperature went down to thirty-five degrees below zero. In the night, we heard a little squeal, and the doorknob moved. As we opened the door, they were licking the doorknob. That was their way of asking if they could come in to get warm by the stove. When they were babies, they slept by the stove; they never forgot that there they would be warm. We let them in. They stood by the stove for a little while and again went out into the cold night.

One cold day, we were moving into the cottage (our winter quarters). We had a heating stove on the cottage porch. Wopsy saw the stove, and he jumped up on the porch and lay down by it, chewing his cud. No doubt, he was wondering why the thing was not putting out heat, but this proved that he knew what a heating stove was when he saw one.

When we started cutting and packing ice from the creek for summer cooling, our helpers were on the job with us. Every few minutes, Wopsy had to have a drink from the hole in the ice where we were cutting. All of a sudden, it happened. He went in headfirst. Otto happened to grab him by the rump just before he went under the ice. After he was out of the ice-cold water, I had to hurriedly take him to the house and dry him out by the stove. As we ran home, ice formed on his hair, and he rattled as if his bones were dry.

I had fun with them all winter. I made a harness for them and taught them to work as a team. Sometimes I had a runaway. Topsy was nice, but Wopsy was a problem. I had jingle bells on the harness. As Wopsy bucked, the bells jingled, and he seemed to enjoy the noise. After a runaway, he stayed out in the timber for a while, but since Topsy did not follow him, he came back as meek as a little lamb and as if nothing had happened.

During summer, if people who lived in the cabins left the door open, they had unexpected company. If they were taking a nap, Topsy and Wopsy licked their faces or started to eat their hair, or they jumped on the bed and lay down, too. But if they happened along at mealtime, this was too bad; they stuck their noses into everything so quickly that it was almost impossible to keep them from eating the food that was within their reach. And then out would come two deer, as somebody was booting them through the door. Then they stood on the porch looking in through the window.

At fifteen months, nature started to call them into the woods and away from me. They stayed in the timber more and more, until, finally, they came home seldom.

The second winter, they stayed out with their wild comrades. After that, they were only partly tame. At mating time, which, in our part of the country, is in late November and early December, the bucks wean the fawns. He does not want them around their mothers. Therefore, he is after them continuously. When he starts after a fawn, he means business. I watched one big buck trying to separate the fawns from the mothers. It was somewhat of a job for him to keep the does from going to the fawns. They all seemed to want to be together. The buck ran at the fawns, his head down, striking at them with his front feet as though he meant to kill them. At this time, he had his antlers, and he did not hesitate to use them. The poor little fawns seemed so frightened. They ran for their lives. When the buck had chased them to his satisfaction, he went back to the does, which he gathered into a bunch and took away in another direction.

During breeding time, he seems to be the master, but during winter, nature takes his antlers away from him. In the spring, when the does are having their young, he is growing new antlers which, while in velvet, are very tender to touch, and the doe can easily handle him because of his sensitive head. No doubt, he would make a nuisance of himself if nature had not seen to it that he has to be a good boy. I have been told that an old buck with a large set of antlers, if in poor condition, will starve to death during the velvet stage because his heavy head makes it impossible for him to feed. The new antlers are very thick and heavy with blood, which later start to harden and dry up into a bone-like structure.

This summer, Topsy and Wopsy are running somewhat together, and frequently we see them in the meadow, but they will not let us pet them now. To me, Topsy and Wopsy will never die. They will always be grazing in one of the many lovely meadows among the silver-tainted spruce, and as I go out for a hike with only my dog, I will always think that the deer that I see are my Topsy and Wopsy.

Now we have a pig-like grunt. This sound I would know anyplace now, but when I came to the mountains to live, little did I know that the grunting that I heard while picking red raspberries was being made by a bear. Had I known, I probably would not have been picking berries, but instead, I would have been moving out of that territory in a hurry. The bear is one animal that is feared by other animals and by many people, and yet seldom do we get to see him. I know that on two different occasions, I was only a few feet from a bear. He saw me first and made his getaway so quickly that I never got a glimpse of him.

On one occasion, I was trailing some horses up a creek. I was making my way through swampy, willow-covered territory where there were many beaver dams. The day was hot. I was now in a canyon where the walls were high and country rough, when suddenly, I heard brush cracking and rocks rolling from the mountainside. Thinking that I had spooked some deer, I went on trailing the horses. I followed their tracks to the opposite side of the canyon from where the animal that I had spooked had gone, so I did not see the tracks that it made.

Topsy and Wopsy Being Grained After a Workout

I had no way of telling what I had spooked. I found the horses on top of a high ridge where they were peaceably standing, head to tail of each other, fanning flies from their bodies. I caught good old Lady, put the halter on her, and started back over the trail to the beaver dams, where I thought the horses would want a drink. But before I got to the beaver dams, the horses stampeded and ran down the canyon.

Lady pulled away from me, and she, too, went down the canyon on a high run, the halter rope slapping from side to side. Now I was curious. I went to the dams to see what had spooked the horses. I found the water riled up, and on the bank, in the mud, there was a big bear track.

"Whoa!" Did I make the most of my opportunity! I, too, hightailed it down the canyon like a deer. On my way up, what I thought to be spooked deer was a spooked bear, and as the horses came by, they still could smell his odor. Horses and cows can detect bear odor from a great distance, and they lose no time in making their getaway.

Another time, I was bringing the milch cows home from the pasture, when suddenly, they stopped and refused to go another step down the trail. Instead, they turned around and ran back into the direction that I was driving them from. By now, I was accustomed to Mr. Bear spooking my animals. I did not see him, but I was certain that he was there someplace. I was only about an eighth of a mile from home. I thought, "What is this bear doing? Is he following me home?" I did not like the idea. I had been enjoying this mountain playground for a long time. Never once was I afraid to go anyplace. He could not spoil it for me now. But what about a third time? Will there be a third time?

Yes, the third time came one very dark night at three o'clock in the morning, right after the Sprucesters had been up for their annual party. Rex barked in the night and awakened Otto. I was too tired to wake. It would have taken much more than the bark of a dog to awaken me. As a rule, I am first to hear a disturbance, and I get up to investigate. But not this time. Rex did not bark anymore, so Otto did not get up. But, in a little while, Otto heard a chicken squawking, and he got up in a hurry.

He took the flashlight and the .22 rifle and went to the chicken house, thinking a skunk or a lynx cat may have gotten the screen door open and gotten into the chicken house. As he went, he pumped a shell into the gun barrel. He flashed the light into every direction, but before he got to the chicken house, there, going along the corral fence behind the chicken house, was a bear.

Otto knew that he could no more than make the bear mad if he shot at him with the .22 rifle, so he quickly started back to the house after his .30-40 rifle. On the way to the house, he discharged the .22, as our policy was to never leave a shell in a gun barrel. With his big rifle ready to fire, he went back to the chicken house, and as he approached, the big black object was in front of the chicken house eating a chicken. As Otto flashed the light on it, the black heap raised up and stood on its hind legs. Otto fired. He missed, but the bear went down on his four feet and started eating again. Otto again came to the house. This time, he was excited. He wanted me to go hold the flashlight so that he could see his mark. He was talking to me. I could hear him, but I could not wake up. What he was saying did not make sense—something about bear and chicken. But all of a sudden, I did wake up. What Otto was saying *did* make sense. The bear had gotten into the chickens.

I jumped out of bed like I had been poked with a hot iron. I stuck my feet into my house shoes. Over my pajamas, I pulled on a pair of jeans and a jacket, and I was ready. Otto had put more shells into the .30-40 rifle, and, for good measure, we took the gasoline lantern for more light. Away we went into the black, cold night.

Sure thing, there he was at the chicken house steps, still eating chicken. Otto kept saying that he could not see, so I held the lantern on top of my head. I pointed the flashlight right at the bear. Otto fired. Nothing happened, only now we could see two big green eyes looking right at us. The green lights immediately went out, but the black heap was still there, moving a little. I said, "He is not dead yet. Give him another one." *Bang* went another shot, and again those big green eyes. Now, I wanted a shot. I just knew that I could hit that bear, but the answer was, "No."

"I will get him this time." We moved closer (to be exact, we were now only forty-five feet from the bear). Otto kept telling me that I was not holding the light so that he could see the bear.

"Why can't you see him?" I asked. "He is just where he was when you started shooting." So he shot again, and again, and always, as he fired, those green eyes looked at us, but they only looked at us for a second. It looked like the bear was badly wounded and that he could only raise his head. But, all of a sudden, he seemed to come to life, and he tore at the chicken as though he wanted to get all that he could of the meat in a hurry. Otto shot again, and the bullet found its mark. Again, the bear stood up on his hind legs. To me, he looked huge, as if standing there in the dim light was Paul Bunyan. But as quickly as the bear stood up, he was gone. I was sick all over, for I was sure that he had been hit. We did not follow him, knowing that a wounded bear is dangerous.

We came home in a hurry. Otto said that he was cold and would go back to bed to get warmed up. I was chilled, too, but I did not want to go to bed. I wanted to go out and see what damage the bear had done. The cows were put into the corral last night. The calves were in the yard. The bear came right through the yard. He could have killed many things. Oh, would daylight ever come!

I started a fire in the cookstove and made some coffee. I drank a cupful. It made me feel warm, and it filled that empty feeling on the inside of me. I was drinking my second cup when I happened to think, "All this time, Rex was not with us!" For a while, I forgot that there might be danger in the darkness. I dashed outside and began calling Rex. He did not come. Now I remembered that Otto had said that Rex barked only once. He must be killed. I did not know what to do. I called again. I flashed the light around in the yard, but I could see no sign of Rex.

I had been waiting for daylight so long. Would it ever come? I drank some more coffee, and I sat there hoping that if Rex heard me calling him, he would come to the kitchen door so I could let him in and be sure that he was all right. I looked out again. Day was breaking. In just a little while, I could see well enough to go out and check on everything. I put on my coat and took the .30-40 rifle and stepped outside carefully, looking all around me before I went out into the yard. Again, I called Rex, but he was nowhere around. I looked for any trace of blood in the yard, but I could find none, so I went to the chicken house.

There, I found the roost torn down. Blood was smeared around. Crippled chickens crouched in corners. Others were coming from where they had scattered in the night. I could not tell how many had been eaten, as I had not kept count on them for some time. Those that were badly hurt, I killed. Others had to take a chance on getting well. Now, I had to check on Otto's shooting. Why couldn't he hit that bear?

I stood where we had stood in the night. I was amazed at how close we really were to the bear. By the bullet marks in the dirt and in the tree roots, I could see that Otto was shooting right at the bear's feet, but I could not be sure that the bear had been hit. There was only a little blood where he was eating the chicken, and that could have been chicken blood. I decided to go in the direction where we thought the bear had gone.

"I may find him," I thought, "if he was hit hard. He may now be dead." I walked across the meadow and into some timber where we had seen bear droppings during summer. By chance, there may be his hideout, and there he may have gone to die. I was as nervous as a child about to recite its first piece. I had gone about a mile, unconscious of the distance, when a noise behind me startled me. I was afraid to look around, but in no more time than I was frightened, I was glad, for it was Rex behind me. He was as glad to see me as I was glad to see him, but he was still frightened from last night. Since Rex was hiding in the timber, the bear must not have been there. I came home.

What had actually happened was that, when Otto went out the first time and saw the bear at the corral, another bear was in the chicken house. As soon as the one at the corral saw Otto, he made his getaway. By his tracks in the soft dirt, I could see that he took out. While the one bear was walking along the corral fence, the other one was in the chicken house getting himself a chicken. While Otto was getting his big rifle, the bear had caught a chicken and had come outside to eat it. Had this happened when I was not so tired, I would have been the one to get up. I would have gone to the chicken house to see what was disturbing the chickens, and I would have walked right into the bear's arms. And to think what story the bear would have had to tell his grandchildren. "One dark night, I went into a chicken house to get me a nice young chicken, and I came out with an old hen!"

After checking on the chickens, I went into the corral to see about the cows, but they were gone. As they went out, each took a section of the corral fence, leaving only one pole across the top. I could see the cows about a quarter of a mile away in a fence corner. Two calves were across the fence from their mothers, and one was still in the yard, so frightened that it did not know what to do. We were weaning the calves, and I was afraid that they would get to their mothers, so I hurriedly came to the house to ask Otto to help me corral the cows. When I got to the house, he was still in bed. I asked him to come help corral the cows, but I did not wait for him to get up. I started out to get the cows that I was most afraid of the calves getting to. When I got to the cows, they were still spooked, but I managed to get a rope on the lead cow. But she was in no mood to go back to where she had seen the bear only a few hours earlier. I tugged on the rope, and step by step, I got her to the corral, but she would not go under the one pole. I coaxed, but she had a mind of her own. I tied her to the pole and started to the chicken house to get an axe that I kept there for emergencies.

With it, I could take down the pole and put the cow back in the corral. On my way after the axe, I came across a bloody trail.

So the bear *was* hit! And he went in exactly the opposite direction from where we thought he had gone. He made about two jumps going west and turned and went north and sat down behind a large coop where he'd left his calling card. Had we followed him, he, no doubt being very mad, would have pounced right on us from behind the coop. But, our good angel told us to go home and wait for daylight. Since we did not follow him, he moved on. I followed the bloody trail over the corral fence, over a large fallen tree, and into some large boulders in back of the cow shed.

I left the cow tied and hurriedly went to the house to tell Otto what I had discovered, but he was gone. So I again took the big rifle, and I went back to follow the bloody trail into the mountain of large boulders. I had the rifle ready to fire should I again see those green eyes.

Carefully, I got up on a large boulder, looking all around me when I suddenly heard a groan that sounded like it came from under the very boulder that I was standing on. I let out a blood-curdling whoop. (I saw Otto coming, but he was yet far away. He had gone after the other cow, and not having her on a rope, they were just going around in a circle. She—like the first one—did not want to go back into the corral.)

And I came zooming down from the top of the boulder with a terrific velocity, and I landed several feet below, still holding the rifle like if I thought it was a rotten egg and it would explode any minute. I scrambled to my feet, looking up and expecting the bear to land right on top of me, not knowing exactly where the sound came from. I began to run, and as I ran, I kept looking back and feeling certain that the bear would pounce on me from someplace. And the first thing I knew, I ran smack into the cow that I had tied to the pole. She let out another groan, but now she was not standing on her four legs; she was almost standing on her head with all four of her feet in the air.

Knowing that a cow in this position would soon die, I put down the gun, grabbed hold of her leg, and started to pull. But I could not move her. I ran to the other side and grabbed another leg. I may just as well have been trying to move one of those large boulders. I could not budge her. I stopped to take hold of her horn and *bang!* Something hit me back there. I grabbed for the part of me that I was sure was missing. Jumping Joseph! Warm, sticky blood! I looked at my hand, expecting to see blood, but what I saw was green.

"Oh, no blood, but disintegrated grass all over my hand and the cow's tail, too. So that's what banged me?"

Another pull at the horn and out of the ground it came, and the cow got up under her own power. And here was Otto asking, "What the hell were you squawking about?"

"Brother," I said. "If you thought you were stanking right in the middle of a wounded bear, you would squawk like hell, too."

I had tied the cow to the one pole on the corral fence that was not knocked down, and in all of my excitement, I forgot about her. While I was scrambling around, she got spooked and jumped over the pole; she had probably seen the bear moving out of the rocks. Being tied, she threw herself and landed on her head, sticking one horn into the ground. She could not get up, and she lay there on her back groaning. It was she that I had heard groaning and not the bear.

I tried to tell Otto what had happened. I told him about the bloody trail that I had been following. I said that the bear must be there someplace. I handed him the rifle, and I said, "Let's go." Rex was now with us, still frightened, but willing to help.

We went into the boulders where only a few minutes ago I had almost killed my fool self. I had never had such a spooky feeling as I had then, looking under boulders and expecting to see a bear under any one of them. No intelligent people would go poking into rocks looking for a wounded bear like we were doing. But I guess we just happened to be dumb and brave, because we were doing just that.

Only the bear was not there. He was now on the move from rock pile to rock pile, no doubt keeping an eye on us all the time. By now, he was probably over his mad spell and was afraid. He had the advantage over us. He did not have to puff and grunt in going over rocks like we did. We were now at a steeply sloped rock. He went over it. If we followed, we, too, would have to go over it. We kept piddling around, trying to climb the slick rock. I thought we were getting beastly energetic.

There was a time when I would not have tried it, but we finally make it over. On the other side were a bunch of large pine trees. In them, on the pine needles, we could see where the bear had been lying down. The needles were bloody, and one large tree had claw marks on it. They, too, were bloody. We could see that the blood was running from his right front foot. (He was probably trying to doctor the wound with pitch from the pine tree.) We had to be on the lookout for him all the time, as we were in rough country. Now Rex was trailing freely. He seemed to know what scent he should follow now that he had a good smell of bear blood. He kept trailing, and we were right after him—here, there, and no place in particular, just meandering around. Now trailing was harder. The ground was hard and dry, and there was less blood.

Finally, we came to a creek. We could see where the bear slid down the bank below a beaver dam, and there he had been lying in the water. And again, the same thing—he was gone. He seemed to stay just one jump ahead of us. (Otto had trouble with his legs; he could go only a short distance at any one time, and he had to rest.) Now, Otto could not keep up with Rex and me, so he said that he was going home, but if I wanted to take the rifle and follow Rex, I could. So I took the rifle, and I had to hurry to catch Rex. He seemed to really be doing business now. The trail was wet, and he could follow it easily. This time, he zigzagged through timber, heading for another creek. I kept a check on him to make sure that he was trailing the bear and not on an expedition of his own. I could follow the bear trail by the water dripping from his body. We were now on the other creek, following over a very narrow trail along a steep bank, about ten feet from the creek bed. I could hardly keep from sliding down. And suddenly, it happened.

I did slide all the way down to the creek bed. (Again, I held the gun as if it were a lighted candle and my life depended on the light.) I had to wait for the dust to settle before I dared move for fear that I was sitting on the bear for sure this time. Carefully, I looked all around me and up to the trail, and there was Rex looking down at me. I could not tell if he was trying to laugh at me or if he was sorry for me, but I did not feel like laughing, for my bones felt like they were twisted into a knot. I stood up.

My legs were not broken. I told Rex, come trail, but I soon realized that I was expecting too much of him. How could he trail anything but me? I had rolled all over the place. No dog could pick up a bear trail there. But, in spite of all of this, he did start to trail only a few feet from where I had fallen.

Beaver lake

There was a large log across the creek about two feet from the water. Rex was fooling around it. I walked over there, and on it were footprints—wet sand on three places and the right front foot still bleeding.

"Jeepers!" Was that a close shave! He must have been there someplace waiting to see if I would bypass him, and when I came rolling down, he probably thought that I was after him. I probably scared him half to death, and he got up and moved in a hurry.

But what he did not know was that I was the one that was scared half to death. Again, I was sure that he was in the lead. Now if we followed him, we would have to go through marshy, willow-covered swamp. I kept looking and hoping that I would see him first and that I would have sense enough to stand up on my two perfectly good feet and shoot him and not go sliding around on my hiney-coop.

We got through the swampy place, but in there, we again found blood, as he had crossed a fallen tree, so we were still on his trail. Finally, we were at the foot of a mountain with huge boulders all around us. The bear could have been behind any one of them. Rex refused to go any farther, and I was no more anxious than Rex was to go on, because I had absolutely no way now of telling where he, the bear, had gone. So I decided to go home.

I was still wearing my pajamas but had long since discarded my jacket, having left it back on the trail someplace. This was hot work, following over and under, walking and sliding. I was wet with perspiration, and after all of the rolling on the ground that I did, I was not too clean. When I got home, Otto looked at me and said, "Did you get him?"

I said, "He almost got me."

I probably looked bad enough to have been in a struggle with something. Now that I was at home, I decently dressed into hiking clothes. No decent woman should be running around after a bear in her pajamas.

The milking was done, and breakfast was on the table, and I was starved. We ate, and I told Otto that I thought it would be a good idea if he went back there with Rex and me; he could ride Lady to the foot of the mountain. Just to have him with us would give a feeling of security. Or, would it, if he could not run? Then he could entertain the bear while Rex and I made the kill. "Oh, yeah!"

This time, we went out to bring in the bear dead or alive—gun, skinning knife, horse, a little dog, and two screwy people. Or the bear may bring us home very much alive. The only reason he would not catch us, he could not see us for the dust.

I took Otto to where we left off. We looked for a long time before we found any more blood, for it seemed that when the bear got to the foot of the mountain, he really took out. The blood drops over the rocks were far apart.

When we got to the top of the mountain, the pine needles were bunched where he ran over them, so he must have really been scared. In many places, the ground was windswept, and no tracks were visible. I would point to the disturbed pine needles and say to Rex, "Trail," and he would scratch the needles and make a bed for himself and lie down. He looked at me as much as to say, "Can't you see I can go no more?" I understood, for I, too, was tired, and I could have bedded down with him for a good rest.

Otto and I tried to decide what to do. It was now late afternoon, so we came home, leaving the job unfinished. Many times since, Rex has acted as though he smelled a bear. I began to think that if that bear was not careful, one of those dark nights, I would run right into him in our backyard.

The enthusiasm the youngsters showed was amazing. They were always ready for another story. But the toss-up was even. I got as much pleasure from being a babysitter/guide as they got out of the little game that I played with them.

The youngsters wanted another story. I said, "Not today. Now we must hurry home." When we got home, mothers were sitting on the porch enjoying themselves for the first time since they had arrived at the place, not having had the children to care for.

Before we were seen, we were heard, and before the poor, worried fathers had a chance to ask me why I took their children into the woods where I could have lost them all, they were overwhelmed. All of the children were safe and sound, and they bubbled over with excitement. Each youngster talked about a different animal, and they all talked at the same time. What they said made sense.

"How do they know all of this? Did they see these animals? How could they have? How so?" Their questions were endless.

The fathers had been out in the woods and along the creek every morning, noon, and evening every day that they had been there, and all that they saw was a little pine squirrel sitting on a branch up in a tree eating nuts out of a pinecone, thumping its feet, scolding in protest, saying, "You are trespassing. Go away." Their very own little children learned all of this in only a part of one afternoon. The fathers came to the conclusion that they must listen, so they all settled down on the porch with the mothers, and the parents were amazed at the knowledge of their children about the creatures of the woods. I withdrew to do my chores, and when I came back, the place was quiet. Hungry children were fed, because little eyes were heavy. After much excitement, the children were ready for bed.

In the evening, the adults came to the lodge, where a brisk fire burned in the fireplace. Chairs were pulled up in a circle in front of the fire, and by its flickering light, songs were sung. And later, someone started a tune on the piano, and there was dancing and card games. In all, it was a nice evening for the adults. No one had to entertain the children; they were all tucked into bed.

And someone wanted to know how I did it. So I told them about my little game that I played with the little children when I took them on a hiking trip through the woods. After the first story, they stuck to me like bees stick to honey, and they followed me like a bunch of little lambs. And I excused myself, for I, too, was tired, and I'd made a promise to the little people that I would tell them about birds and trees the next day.

One of the many wonderful little persons that has been to our place is Jill a little four-year-old fellow. Standing in a shower with outstretched hands, smiling and letting the raindrops fall into his little palms, he looked up, saying, "I like the raindrops. They make the grass smile." In that little heart, there was something big. Visiting at our place with his mother and father, he was concerned, because it was getting late, and at home, they had chores to do.

I said, "What chores do you have to do?"

He said, "I feed the chickens and gather the eggs."

"The chickens have gone to bed by now," I said. "They will not be laying or eating anymore today."

"But I must gather the eggs when I get home, because if they are left in the nest overnight, they will freeze," he told me. He had a sense of responsibility though only four years old. By no means was he a sissy. He had an old horse that he was learning to ride, and he could rope and tie up a calf. Oh, well, so what if the calf was a pet, and what if it did lie down as soon as he put a rope around its neck? He was learning young to be a cowboy.

4

MANNA IN THE WILDERNESS

I get bogged down in my work, so I think I will turn on the radio. I hear the familiar voice of my favorite announcer coming from my special radio station, saying fifteen minutes of vocal music; I think this is just what I need. Noise, not music, starts pouring from the radio, and what is it? Something about Rag Hop. There is no harmony. So what do I get? A picture of a dirty rag on a stick. I've been looking at a dirty rag on a stick all morning. I am cleaning house. Disgusted, I turn the radio off, and I wonder what this so-called modern music and singing is doing to a young mind. The music is horrible, if one could call that music. So all that I got out of the fifteen minutes was much noise and a lot of flat blab, blab. I think the radio wonderful; it is our only source of entertainment and news during winter when we are snowed in. But, by comparison, why ruin something beautiful with this blood-curdling entertainment? A few drops of dirty water will pollute a bucketful. I may have lived up in the mountains too long to appreciate some of the modern things of today, but I do not feel that I am missing too much. Some things that I do, do not make sense to other people.

For exercise to take off a few pounds, I do not have to burn the candle at both ends pumping an artificial bicycle or riding a dummy horse. I work hard, and I eat when I am hungry; the rest takes care of itself.

There were times when I did not see anyone but Otto all winter. Though our trips after the mail during winter are few and far apart, Otto always has a visit in a way. He stops at the ranch along the way to the mailbox. As a rule, there are people one can visit with, weather permitting. Much of the time, our papers, during winter, were six weeks old when we got them, and at that time, we had no radio. When Otto came home with the mail, I would ask, "What's new down the line?"

He would say, "I forgot to ask." Next trip down, I would remind him to ask about the well-being of the neighbors.

People say, "Certainly you cannot live alone all winter!" But we are not alone; our animals are a part of our lives. Nature holds the secret to happiness, and no one has been able to take it from her. Here, one can find what one seeks—love, passion, peace, contentment, and relaxation.

Love among the creatures of the forest who make it their home is beautiful. Their courtship is enchanting; their love for home and family is something we human beings could pattern after. The song of a robin to his mate while she builds her nest early each morning and late into the night is so beautiful. How many times I have sat by my window to fill my heart with this entity.

I enjoy clean fun, a job well done, and I enjoy giving my love to animals, be they man or beast. Roam with me in make-believe. Over my hills, along my streams, through my forest, smell the sweet scent of pine. Stand in the breeze, and let it blow through your hair. Soak in the sunshine, and try to feel God's presence as I have over the many years that I have lived at Silver Spruce. I sense this, sometimes daily, sometimes strongly. And this is why my world is beautiful.

I am filled with desire for living. Almost everything I do is fun. There is no more demarcation between work and play, except if one does not like to work. Some people consider cooking hard work—not for me as long as I have something to cook, and there has never been a time when I had nothing. If the worst should happen, we always could find and kill a porcupine; they are edible, though we have never had to eat them.

If the weather is bad, we stay indoors at such time; we catch up on reading and letter writing. Especially during winter, people on the outside like to get letters from us; they like to know if we are alive. They seemed surprised when we tell them that we haven't had as much cold, mushing snow many times all day because we enjoy being out in it; but this is why we are healthy.

We have learned to work together. If we are working on Otto's job, then I am a helper, and if we work on my job, Otto is the helper. We are never either one a boss. We are only equal partners. As long as we do not interfere with one another, we can get along. We took each for better and for worse, and so we must take the bitter with the sweet. Life is not roseate for everybody. There are poor millionaires and rich millionaires. Many things money cannot buy, and I feel that what we have, no money could buy—contentment and satisfaction of a big accomplishment. Wherever we look, we see things that we did with our own hands. We appreciate what we have, because it was not handed to us on a golden tray. Earned money gives most pleasure, because we know its value. We have had laughter and sorrow up here, but there is no place where there is all laughter and no tears. Sometimes we are so sure of our side, but when we hear the other side of the story, we see we have no ground the devil would care about; never did two wrongs make one right.

I do not say that we must compensate the devil to be able to live together. We have never had to hide the guns or throw the shells away, though we live up here alone, winter after winter. The little things we do for one another mean so much more to us than the more extravagant things that we would do for show only. To me, it is something special if Otto comes home from a stroll over the hills, or when he brings the cows home in the evenings, and he hands me a little flower that he has picked, and he asks me in his nice voice, "Have you seen any of these flowers this spring? Isn't it beautiful?"

There is one thing that we cannot do in our part of the country during winter, and that is to sit by a window and watch people go by. If we were to see somebody pass by our window, I suppose we would drop dead of surprise or otherwise, but here, too, is an advantage. We do not have to draw our shades. We may have to be careful that we do not get lost in a snowstorm or out in the rugged mountains, but on the other hand, we do not have to be afraid of being run down by a reckless driver should we forget first to look left and right before crossing the yard. If I want to jump out of bed and hightail it to the little house on the hill some bright sunny morning with the temperature at zero, my nightie fanning in the breeze, who cares? This wakes up the old pumper and starts up circulation. Modesty? Oh, yes, we have that, too. We are as dignified as you please if we have to be. It may not be peaches and cream, but we can do it.

We are not bored with neighbors, for we live far enough apart that we are happy to see one another. I do not pretend to know all of the answers to why we do things and enjoy them. It surely is not because we do not know better. We lived the bigger part of our lives in civilization. However, I was never a lily of the field, neither do they toil nor spin. But once in a while, believe it or not, I put on high heels, and I go to town, and I even get a new hairdo once each year—though I go barelegged and I wear my old shoes until we have gone through the six gates, since it is my job to open them. After we are through the last gate, I start putting on my one and only pair of nylons, sticking my knee into Otto's face while he is trying to drive. If he dodges fast enough and swings the car hard enough, then his nose has missed my knee, and I have missed the seat, and I find myself sitting down on the floor still juggling my foot and a shoe.

Going home, I start changing footwear long before we reach the first gate. I am not being apologetic. I only have one pair of good hose at a time. This is why I cannot take chances on snagging them.

If we go to town after the road has been partly snowed in and we are not sure that we can get through without me getting out to push, then over my shoes I put on a pair of four-buckle overshoes, and under my dress, I pull on a pair of jeans, and I let my dress hang over them. I always have to remember to take the jeans off before we get to town. But should I sometime forget, I think I would look rather cute going down the street with my pantaloons showing under my dress. After World War II, we got a war surplus light plant and a snow weasel; this is a vehicle that rides on top of the snow.

In the snow weasel, there are two single seats, one behind the other. When this perambulator was in running order, I rode in the cockpit, and Otto did the driving. I guess I was the tail-gunner, only my job was not as that of a tail-gunner's; I sure I was not one, for my job was to scramble out every time one of the tracks started slipping and put it back into place. I got so good at this job that I could do it with the wink of my eye. I would lay a flat iron this way and that way and say, "Okay, pull up," and the track simply jumped back into place.

During winter, we parked our car six miles down the road, and it stayed there until spring. From home to the car, we traveled in the weasel, and from the car to town, we went first class. The snow weasel had lost its top long before we got it, so we just tied a tarpaulin over the iron bows that once held up the top, and we rode with the tarpaulin flopping and banging as if somebody was trying to flag down a train. When people down the line saw us coming, they all had respect for us; we were a part of Uncle Sam's army. We were referred to as the army coming. Or could it be that they had respect for the snow weasel? After all, it was once a part of Uncle Sam's army. Whoever, or what for, the consideration, I always felt like I was Uncle Sam himself riding in the rumble seat.

Even though I had to get in acrobatically, if I started in feet first, I got my head mixed up with the top. If I got on my hands and knees and I landed in the bottom of the weasel on my face, I knew I was in. Had I been a soldier on a battlefield, the enemy would have had a good target and always in the same place. I can say this much—that's the gosh-darndest vehicle to get into. One riding in the thing spends most of the time in transit between the top and the bottom being tossed helplessly in the air like popcorn popping. I would no more than get my carcass parked into the rumble seat and out I came, only to bang my head on a bowed iron in the top. I have not yet decided if those irons were put there to hold up the top or to bang people on the noggin and put them to sleep while they are being helplessly carried around in the appaloosa.

I have another job where I ride like royalty. I help Otto put up hay. We have a tractor. It is not one of those graceful little things that you can turn on a dime and can run under a cow with. Ours is different. It's one that Mr. McCormick and Mr. Leering made. They must have had an awful lot of material they wanted to get rid of, so they kept adding to this tractor until they had an iron monster. It takes an acre of land when one has to turn it. You start pulling long before you start turning. I mean pulling with both hands on one side of the steering wheel, and if you pull hard enough, it may turn. But you always warn the trees ahead of you to be sure to get out of the way just in case you did not pull hard enough.

It feeds automatically. The more you want it to stop, the harder it goes. And all this time, I am the tail-gunner on the mowing machine. I am that sure in this case, I am the tail-gunner, because I work things with my feet and my hands, too. I kick this, and I pull that, and the clamor starts. I am supposed to watch if the thing is cutting all of the hay down and remember where all of the rocks are in the tall grass and raise the sickle bar so that I do not cut one of those big rocks in two. Otto drives the iron monster, and it pulls the mowing machine.

The little creek picked the middle of the meadow to run through. On one side, the meadow is almost level; the other side is a little up and down. One place is so steep that when we come down, the mowing machine and I come down sideways. I grab the seat with one hand, and with the other hand something I should not have grabbed, and something happens. We are not cutting hay. Otto looks back and says something to me that I cannot hear, because there are too many things banging around, including me. Finally, we stop. My head is spinning. My fanny is burning, and Otto wants to know, "Why did you not tell me we were not cutting grass?" Fantastic!

After what seems like several days, or it may be just two, we are through mowing. Now we have to rake the hay. We have one of the oldest and most dilapidated hay rakes in the country—or maybe in the whole world. The wheels are both bent this way and that way. They are loose at the axle. Riding it is like riding one of those crazy things in a carnival called the Whip. You start going and *bang,* you run into yourself going the other way. Our rake is like this, only much worse. I dump it with my hand while ⊠ aim I hang on to the seat with the other hand, and I mean hang on to the seat, because part of the time I am sitting on it. I lean forward as far as I can, and I push a lever, and I loose the hay that has been riding behind me. If I am lucky, I stay on, and we pick up some more hay.

We just keep going around and around until all of the hay is raked. All this time, my innards are bouncing from side to side and up and down, and my stomach is about to fly out of my mouth. Then we haul the hay in on a wagon. The wagon is so old that we have the rims wired onto the wheels. One time, a wire busted, and one of the rims came skipping, bouncing, and rolling past us as though it did not belong to us.

"What the hell!" Otto said.

"Your wheel rim broke loose, and it's running away," I told him. I jumped from the load of hay and started after it. We went through a marsh that is too wet to mow and where the grass is very tall. We headed for the little creek. Finally, I grabbed the rim, but it was too heavy, and it was rolling too fast. After much struggling, I subdued it and went back to the wagon. (Sure, I had the rim. Didn't I run like a wild rabbit to catch it?) We pried the wagon up and put the rim back on the wheel before it fell apart. (Oh, yes, the wagon was full of hay.) This sort of thing happens a lot, and we go until something else happens, which, as a rule, is not too long.

I build the stack while Otto throws the hay on my head. When all of the hay is one pile, it either leans one way or the other. It is never straight, but that's how I build a haystack.

We have one more old thing on the place besides me, and that's Lady. Yes, Lady. She is twenty-four years old that we know of, and I think the man from whom we bought her forgot to put in all of her years when we got her. She is still a very good horse. She is one of those easy keepers. Everything she eats goes to fat. (Food affects me that way, too.) Lady's motto is "Get there any way you can—over, under, or between." If we do not watch her, she takes the skin from our knees, bumps our heads on branches, and stumbles over everything that she comes to. Riding her is like riding a hobbyhorse with a broken spring.

One day, I was riding her down after the mail. She got spooked at one of her own piles that she stopped to make in the road. (Yes, she always stops to do that.) I saw it long before we got to it; how could I have missed it? It looked like a young bear sitting in the road, but I thought she saw it, too, so I just sat in the saddle like mush. All of a sudden, she decided to jump away from her own dung. First, she jumped straight up and then to the side, and I flew up with the first jump. When I came down, she was not there, so I landed a bunch of rocks and busted my elbow … yes, and *that,* too. This was when Lady was still young—about three years ago.

We love Lady very much. She is so understanding. If we are not at the haystack in the morning as soon as she thinks we should be, she comes to the fence and calls us. She lives with the cows, so we call her horse-cow. Of the original animals, there are only three of us left: Otto, Lady, and I. Slats, our second cat, left us last fall. He had lived to a ripe old age.

Otto's house is getting very old, too. It needs a new foundation and a new roof, and the walls need to be straightened up. It's as cold as the out of doors. The chimney is dropping out. On windy days, we have to tie down the furniture so that it does not fly out through the cracks, and the house itself looks like it is trying to curtsy to royalty. We cannot burn it down, because we need it. I do not see how we can rebuild it, for time flies like clouds in a storm, and our birthdays pass like fenceposts when traveling at a high speed. Otto is shrinking by the day. I am spreading out all over the place, and we both look like old prunes.

And I am as mad as a chained-up hound dog when I hear that some of our very own American people are defrauding our government and that some people enjoy the goodness of America when their hearts are in another land. I wonder why Uncle Sam doesn't just give them a kick in the pants and tell them to take what he kicked to where their hearts are. It hurts me deeply to hear about the improbability in our government, because I help to defend and support it, and I wonder where everybody was when Uncle Joe had his hand in Uncle Sam's pocket. Next to God, I love America, and to have my country hurt is hurting me, and I just don't like to be hurt. To have such ingratitude is like sticking a knife into my heart.

There are always a few discompoops in this world of ours. They even crucified our own Jesus. Now they are trying to crucify our heritage. In America, as a whole, we are not a bad bunch of people. We have been a big brother to our friends across the pond. It takes many spokes to make a wheel; it seems now that everybody wants to be the wheel. People are made up like a nice pie; there is the upper crust, the filling, and the bottom crust. Without the filling, the upper crust is not so good, and the bottom crust is worthless.

Otto and I have lived up here so long that everything is a part of our lives. Our place, to us, is like a child that we have reared from infancy. We have combed through the ugly and rough tangles until now we have a smooth road to travel over. To some people, this kind of life would not appeal. To us, it has been very wonderful. For one thing, we both enjoy the out of doors. Before we knew this place existed, we went out into the mountains at every opportunity. Otto had a Hupmobile Light touring car. I had a Model T coupe. When we went places that we did not think the Hup could go, or if we were in doubt of it, I took my puddle jumper. We could always make it through in it.

If we came to a creek that had no bridge, we could build one by throwing in a few rocks and brush, and if there was no road, we took out across country. If the hill was too steep, Otto could always hang out on the upper side. When I took my car, Otto took the lunch and vice versa. We went skylarking over pieces where only a horsebacker would go.

And then this opportunity came up. When we were starting up, at times it looked like a foolish undertaking, but, for some reason, we never felt that we could not make a go of it. It took much hard work before we had an income from the place.

What money we have saved up from our store jobs was being used up fast. We had grown into a few head of stock. We decided to ship some of them, because we were in need of money to buy winter supplies. We had to stock up for six months. That took a lot of money at one time. Going to town during the winter was out.

One evening, I was washing dishes. I watched Otto bring in the nine head of stock that we had. They were nice and fat, and they were all playing as they went along. That evening, we talked about shipping five head, and we were trying to decide which five we could part with. They were all pets. We hated to sell any of them. Finally, we decided on one old cow and some two-year-olds. This would give us all of the money that we would need for food and some extra for feed for the four cows and three horses that we had to winter. We had a good feeling. It looked like everything was going to work out fine for the winter. Next summer, there would be a little guest money coming in.

The next morning, Otto went out to milk while I got breakfast. But no more than he went out and he was back in the house; he looked as though he had seen a ghost. I was sure nothing dreadful had happened, but I was afraid to ask. Finally, Otto said, "Something very bad happened last night. Seven of our head of cattle are dead."

We could not eat. I got the breakfast on the back of the stove. I did not see how I could go out to the corral, but I had no choice. Otto had to have help. When I got to the corral, the dead critters were lying as if they were still sleeping, their hands on their sides. What killed them, we did not know, but death seemed to have come instantly.

The headache was terrific. I did not see them as dead cows, but as our pets, playing as they went to bed for the last time. We took the two remaining cows out of the corral, and we cared for them. They appeared to be all right, but one later lost her calf prematurely.

We had to drag all of the dead cows away, so we hooked up the team, and all day, we dragged dead cows around. We took each carcass to a place where we could make coyote sets around them. We could get something out of them as coyote and cat bait. Now our plans were all shattered. We had no money for winter supplies.

But somehow we got along. I had canned a lot of vegetables that summer out of our garden, and I had butter packed and cream canned. The little money that we had on hand we used to buy a few staple groceries.

Otto had an old heavy overcoat. Out of it, I made mittens and pacs to wear in our old galoshes. We both could keep our hands and feet warm. I patched all of our wool socks and what other old clothes we had. A few more patches would make little difference. We made out nicely.

All winter, we worked like troopers. We each had a trapline that covered several miles. Most of each day we were gone, each in a different direction, looking after our traps. When we got home late in the afternoon, we had so much to tell each other. Some things that happened on the trapline were funny; some were almost tragic. We each were proud of what good accomplishment we may have made. Our evenings were really important. We each tried to do a good skinning job on what fur we had.

Our efforts paid off. Many times, with our fur check, we got an extra five-dollar check as a reward for a well-prepared pelt. In all, we won five such awards, and I won a prize of $150 for a well-prepared lynx cat pelt. We were really happy to get this extra money, and at Christmas, we got a card from my sister, Winnie, and with it a couple of five-dollar bills and a note saying, "Buy yourselves something. I did not know what you would like."

Little did she know that the money looked better than anything that she could have bought for us. With it, our garden seed problem was solved. The money was put into the seed catalogue, and the catalogue was put away until it was time to order seeds.

For a long time, we felt the loss of the stock. One sacrifice after another had to be made. We appreciated more than ever what we had, but those were not the only losses that we had. As time went on, we lost many more cows, horses, and the two wonderful dogs that we valued highly.

5

FOOD PRODUCTION

It is surprising how fast vegetables grow in high altitude. We cannot put seeds into the ground too early, yet we must put them in as soon as the growing season has started. We wait for Mother Nature to give us the go-ahead sign before we start planting. As soon as the aspen trees start to unfold their foliage, it is time for us to start planting.

The time varies. Sometimes we can start to plant in the middle of May, and sometimes we must wait until June. We have only three months in which to grow a garden, and this we must do without irrigation. Since frost settles into low places along a stream, we must put the garden on a hill, where we could get water by pumping only. For moisture, we must depend on rain, which we do not always get when we need it. We manage to grow a nice garden, though, by taking everything into consideration.

Our vegetables are all of excellent quality. We grow peas, corn, beets, radishes, lettuce, carrots, rutabaga, pumpkins, cabbages, celery, onions, and potatoes. All of these vegetables are most delicious, because they grow fast; they get enough moisture out of night air to keep growing. We are eating potatoes six weeks from planting time. We select seed from the best hills and keep them in the cellar where the temperature is just above freezing all winter. At least two weeks before planting, we bring out the seeds that we will plant and keep them in the house where it is warm, and they sprout nicely before we put them into the ground. If we wait to plant after the ground has warmed up, seeds come up fast, and the plants are strong; this is because the seeds have not lost their vitality. I can the peas, corn, and beets. We keep carrots, rutabagas, and potatoes until spring in the cellars; we can also keep cabbage for a while, but it will not keep all winter; we make much of it into sauerkraut. We live out of our garden the year round; we eat vegetables fresh and later out of jars.

At one time, we had all of the wild raspberries we could pick; I canned juice, and I canned whole berries. This way, I could use either as I needed them. Out of fresh berries, besides regular pie, I made an open-face pie out of raised sweet dough. I rolled the dough about one-half-inch thick and fitted it into a pie tin. This I filled with raspberries and put one-half cup of sugar over the top. As it baked, juice from the berries baked into the crust and made delicious eating. I served this with a pitcher of heavy cream.

Besides having moisture worries, we have many rodents, such as pocket gophers, rockchucks, porcupines, and mice. They all eat vegetables. But the deer are our big problem. We cannot kill them, for they are protected by law, and I do not think we would kill them if we could, because our guests enjoy seeing them around the place and so do we, but we have not yet figured out how to keep them from eating our garden. We cannot put up a fence high enough to keep them from jumping over.

I put out some flags, thinking that the waving would spook them, but by their tracks, I could see that they went right up to the flags, because they were curious. I strung wires from post to post, and I put cowbells on the wire, thinking that if they ran into the wire, the bell would ring and scare them away. But again, by their tracks, it looked like that while one rang the bells, the rest had a square dance all over the garden, and after the dance, they all had lunch. This time, I was sure I had figured a way to keep them out; I took a tarpaulin to the garden and made a pup tent. In it, I made a bed for one cat, one dog, and myself. I did not think the cat or dog would keep the deer out of the garden, but at least they could keep mice or bear out of my bed. To me, this seems logical; if a deer smells human odor, he would stay his distance. No—not the deer we have. It didn't work. While I slept, the deer ate practically everything in the garden. They no doubt thought that I was there to watch the dog so that he would not chase them.

READY FOR A HIKE INTO THE MOUNTAINS

Finally, where I had the bells I put lanterns and kept a light burning all night. My garden was as bright as Broadway; this did the trick.

The hopper problem was licked by getting some turkeys; I know it must seem foolish for us to go to so much trouble to grow a few vegetables, but think about the good nutrition we get out of vegetables that are taken out of the garden and eaten in only a few minutes. They do not lose vitamins like the vegetables that have been knocking around for days before they get to the table. So what's a little trouble in comparison? It gives so much satisfaction to be at least in part self-sustaining. I think this is why I enjoy working. When I can our food, I feel so proud as I stack full jars into the cellar; they are vegetables that we grew and canned so quickly after we picked them that they had all of the goodness in them that they got out of our rich soil, pure air, and sunshine.

Our garden location was covered with huge sage brush and was for years used as a sheep bed ground. The sage brush, giving the sheep protection from wind, made this a favorite sleeping ground. The droppings over many years decomposed with the sage brush leaves, and this made the soil very rich and mellow. I think this enables us to grow vegetables of excellent quality.

One year, I decided that I wanted a strawberry bed. I worked like a Trojan preparing the ground, and as soon as the berries began to ripen, a very sweet mother grouse and her babies moved in. After that, I never got another ripe berry. This was a covoy that lived in the yard because they were protected from the hawks. The berries did not mean as much to me as they did to the the grouse.

The berries struggled on their own for a few years, but when we got Topsy and Wopsy, they ate the vines to the ground. At that time, we had to give up growing a garden, but now that Topsy and Wopsy have gone out with the wild deer, we are again trying to grow a garden. We get a few things, and the deer get the rest. I guess this is one of those give-and-take games that we must play as we go through life.

During summer, there are times when we have more milk than we can use. At such times, I can cream and pack butter for winter use. We have learned that, up here, the winters are too long and severe for cows to give milk and withstand the cold. By November, I have all of the cream and butter packed that we will need, so we dry the cows up. This gives them a chance to build up before spring storms start coming.

All winter, they have access to a large barn, but they are fed out in the open where, on nice days, they spend much of their time browsing and sunning. When there is a bad blizzard, they eat their hay and go up to the barn to chew their cud and to rest. The first two winters we had cows up here, we tried milking them all winter. We soon learned that this was hard on the cows and on us also. We decided that if meat can be successfully canned at home, why could not cream? I went to work on trying out proper pressure and processing time. In no time, I was canning cream to last us all winter.

We seldom have venison. Otto or I are not killers. We kill when we have to kill. Sometimes during winter, we had no meat, and working hard, I thought I would be the brave hunter and get us some meat. I would go out hoping that I would not see too many deer in one bunch; I always seemed to have a hard time finding one alone. I would see a few does and a buck or two with them. I could not kill one and let the rest see it die, so I went on, still looking for a lone one. Sometimes I did find a lone one, but it was too pretty; no, I could not kill it, either. The deer lived, and we ate beans.

When I first started to hunt, sometimes I trailed the deer backward. In deep snow, I could not tell which way the deer traveled. Now I can tell by the way his tracks slant. Sometimes I would trail a deer for what seemed like hours, and when finally I would come to a place under a large spruce tree where the snow was only one or two inches deep, I could see that I had been going in the wrong direction. Now I know that if his toes point to the east, I do not go west to find him; I really think now I could tell which way a deer went even if he was sliding on his head. How? He does not spit those little marbles out of his mouth when they lay clear on the trail. I know the deer was going away from them.

I have killed a few deer over the many years that I have lived in the mountains. One winter, we had two hogs to butcher. I wanted to try pork and venison sausage, but I had no venison. Knowing that I would have to get venison if I wanted it, I went out with a heart of stone. Nothing would stop me this time. Again I saw deer. In one place, a big buck was lying down with does grazing around him. I looked at the buck through the gun sights. I couldn't do it. So again I went on and on, and to my surprise, I looked and right before my eyes was a lone four-point buck grazing, and he had not seen me. I took a good aim, and he came down without knowing what hit him. I dressed him out, and I went home so proud that I almost popped my shirt buttons. We had deep snow; Otto could not be out in it, because his legs were giving him trouble, so he could not help get the deer in.

Now that I had meat, I would find a way to get it in. I got Lady and saddled her, and then I put the harness on over the saddle, a singletree I hung on one side, a rope on the other. Lady was in an ugly mood; she did not want to go out in the deep snow. If I could get her to where I was going, I would be lucky. And if I didn't hang onto the halter rope, she would come home even before I was ready. Of all the jobs she had to do, packing in a deer was wickedness itself. When we got to the deer, I let her get a good look at it so that she would not know it was a dead deer. I am sure that she would rather the deer had been alive; that way, she would not have to help get it in.

I tied her to a tree; here she could stand until I was ready to go. By now, it was late afternoon, and I was so cold that I felt I could spit ice cubes. I thought, "If Lady will only work with me and not against me, we may get home before I freeze." I fastened the deer by its horns to the singletree. The singletree I fastened to the traces. I thought that pulling a deer in this manner would be easier. I thought, "Now I am all set to go if I can get on Lady's back. I must be careful not to get tangled in the many things I have hanging all around her." I untied her and tried to hang onto the halter rope while I tried to get on, but she did not want to wait. By then, I was too cold to swing into the saddle quickly. I had to figure a way to keep her tied until I was settled on her back. I got a long pole, and I tied the halter rope to one end of it. I let this end rest in the tree crotch; I tied the other end of the pole to the saddle horn. In this manner, Lady was still fast. If she pulled forward, the pole held her back; she would not pull back, because the deer was behind her.

Finally, I was on her back, feet in the stirrups; I was ready to start for home. I pulled the pole back, and away we went with smiles of fortune, snow flying in a fog behind us. Lady soon settled down; pulling a deer with a rider on her back and going uphill was hard work. As soon as she stopped to rest, I would drop the pole, which I carried in one hand. It took us hardly any time to get home; Lady had settled down, and she was walking like a lady should, while I sat on her back like a puffed-up toad.

I rode right to the kitchen door, and when Otto came out, I was really flushed with victory. I unsaddled Lady and fed her. Now I got a tarpaulin, spread it on the kitchen floor, and we skinned the deer on it. The meat was perfect; I only shot a small hole just back of the shoulder, the bullet going through his heart and coming out in front of the other shoulder.

While the venison was curing, we made preparations to butcher the hogs. I went down to the ranch and asked the mister there if he would help butcher; he said that he would. Now with the hogs hanging in four halves, I felt like a millionaire. The mister would not take pay for helping, so we shared some of our meat with him. I cleaned the hog casings, and I stuffed them with half pork and half venison sausage meat. Besides this sausage, I made liver sausage, head cheese, bacon, and hams; now I really felt meat rich.

Working together, nothing seems a problem. Alone, one must take precautions. Otto seems to have even more trouble when working alone; being so very independent, he invariably takes on a job much too big for him to do alone. Now and then, he comes home a little battered, but somehow he gets the job done.

One day, he came home with his face looking like uncooked beef steak.

He had been working with rock; he looked as if one of those big rocks came up and hit him right on the nose—and that's just what had happened. Only the rock did not come up by itself; Otto had it in his hand. He had pried a very large rock loose, but it was still in its nest; he wanted to roll it over, turning it with a large bar until he had a high point on top for better leverage. Sitting face level with the rock, bracing himself, he started to pull on the high point, pulling harder and harder. Suddenly, the gibbosity broke off, and poor Otto hit his face with a handful of rock.

To find out how Otto was hurt when he is on a job alone, I must seem unconcerned; I start tying little pieces of the story together until I have the whole. One time, he came home when putting up hay to tell me that he had swallowed a fly. I said, "Don't worry, darling; the thing is probably digested by now."

"But I feel sick," he told me.

So I put my beloved to bed. Almost immediately, he was up again and saying that he was hungry. I thought, "This is a game we are playing, and I don't feel like playing a game." So I said, "What do you want to eat?" He wanted spinach. Now I knew it was a game, because I have to go one eighth of a mile, in hot sun, to the garden to pick spinach. I picked what seemed like a washtub full; I thought to myself, "I will make you eat spinach until you will never want to look at spinach." I had it ready in double-quick time, and I was going to see that he ate it. How much did he eat? Exactly one quart, cooked and packed, with no water on it. Then he really went to bed and stayed there. I was worried. After eating a quart of spinach, how long could he stay in bed? I tiptoed in, and I found him sound asleep. I made a close inspection to be sure that everything was all right. To my horror, I saw a face as pink as a newborn mouse. I woke him up, and I said, "Darling, you have the measles."

"Hell, no! I am too old to have measles."

And I said, "Remember, my love, I've been telling you it's all in your head."

I was being so nice to him; he was practically knee deep in honey. But I was still worried about the quart of spinach. And the first thing I knew, he was out walking around in the yard. I tried to rush him back to bed, and I warned him, if the measles go in, "You will be even older than that." But I saw that he was heading for the Johnnie, so I gave up. There is no use in worrying; when this is over, something else will happen. Never a dull moment at our house.

Today I must do the evening chores alone, so I take the big job first. I start the cows to the corral so that I can get the milking done. The cows are too full of young green grass. They look like a piggy bank with four squirts sticking out under them. The hill to the corral is too hard to pull, so they take a few steps, and they rest and chew the green grass some more. I dash from one to the other to keep them moving; if I let them stand to chew their cud, we will never get to the corral. How many cows are there? We milk four. The rest are everything; some are steers, three- years -old, some are heifers, and one is an honest-to-goodness bull. He is really nice, but I do not trust him any farther than I could throw him by his tail. In all, there are ten of the bovine. I am about to run my legs off trying to keep them all moving. Finally, a nice elderly gentleman, who is sitting on the cottage porch watching all this, takes pity on me—or the cows—and he comes to help me put all of the cattle into the corral. What he does not know is that one never walks behind a cow full of young green grass; you walk to one side. The gentleman is pushing the cow too hard, so she stops to cough, and at the same time, she backfires, and the gentleman gets it full force right on his chest. He stops to look at his chest, and by now, the mess is down to his knees. I pretend not to see. Now he is showing his chest to his wife. I cannot hear what she says to him, but when I look again, he is heading for the creek with a bundle under his arm.

At last, I have all of the stock in the corral; now I must sort them. The one squirts goes to the upper corral, the four squirts stay in the lower corral where there is a milking shed. Why do we bring in all of the squirts? Otto is afraid that they will be lonesome in the pasture by themselves. Now I settle down to milk four cows. A young fellow who came to watch wants to know how I can sit on a one-legged milk stool; I tell him that I hold on to the handles. He says, "These are faucets the cow turns on to get rid of the milk." I agree that they are faucets, and I keep squirting the milk into the bucket. Now he wants to know why some cows have only one squirt. Little girls are not so interested in squirts. Little boys probably hope to be ranchers someday; they would probably know more about squirts than little girls do, anyway.

At last, I am finished milking, and I feed some of the milk to the calves out of a calf-feeding bucket. And still there are more questions; some I cannot answer, and there are times when we do not take youngsters to the corral.

At last, we are heading for the house, and the little fellow says that he has it all figured out. He thinks that I feed the milk to the calves when they are little, then when they are big, I pump it out.

Suddenly, I think of my poor Otto and the quart of spinach. Finally both Otto and I are in the house. I want to know how everything came out. He says, "Fine." I wonder how I could live without my Otto.

Summers go too fast. Winter comes too soon. Now I snowshoe after the mail, because I keep warmer walking than riding. I must start in the morning just as soon as I can see the trail; if I go all the way to the mailbox, by the time I get back home, I have snowshoed thirteen miles. Coming home, I come uphill all the way with a sack of mail across my shoulders, and when finally I reach home, I am really used up.

When Otto and I lived and worked in Glenrock, we enjoyed going out into the mountains. At every opportunity, we drove out into the country. Hiking is not new to me. I love it. Otto is quite a rock hound, so when I went out into the mountains with him, I always expected to walk a few miles over rocks and hills, into canyons, up on the other side, over another ridge and another, always thinking that the rock Otto wanted to look at was just over the next ridge, but many times, it was miles away.

When we came back to town, I was so tired that I was never sure if I could walk the few steps up to my apartment. And come Saturday, Otto would stop in at the store to ask what I had in mind for the next day. The conversation would start out something like this:

"What will you be doing tomorrow?"

"Oh, about the same as I do every Sunday. I will go to church in the morning, and I have nothing special for the rest of the day," I would say.

Otto would say, "So-and-so brought in a rock that looks good. I thought we could drive out to the see the prospect. I will be ready when you get back from church." By this, I understood he wanted an early start. "We can take a nose-bag." That meant that we would be eating someplace by a creek, and we would be most likely cooking up a big meal.

Then I would ask, "Who shall we ask to go along?"

The answer was always the same. "Ask who you want to."

So I would get busy on the phone and call some of our friends, and everything was set for Sunday.

After each camping trip, the grub box was cleaned out, salt and pepper cans refilled, cornmeal and coffee checked, the lard can filled and put into the icebox, and the grub box was put into its cubbyhole, ready for our next trip.

Saturday evening, Otto would come up with an armful of groceries, and I would put in a few, and we were all set for another trip. Sunday morning, when I got home from church, as a rule, Otto had everybody and everything in his car and was waiting in front of my apartment. As I went hurriedly upstairs, I unsnapped and unfastened everything that I dared unsnap, and as I stepped into my apartment, my clothes dropped to the floor. I stepped out of my dress and into my hiking breeches, boots, and a pull-on sweater, and I was off. By the time I reached the outside door, I was all buttoned up and ready, and before I had time to park my fanny, the car was moving. We were on our way, never knowing where we were going or when we would be back.

After we started coming up to our mountains, we never came alone. We always took some of our friends. Occasionally, we caught a nice mess of trout, and we cooked them over an open fire along the creek and, in addition to trout, we cooked bacon, eggs, and we fried a skilletful of potatoes and made a big pot of coffee.

First, the bacon and eggs were cooked, and in the bacon fat the fish were fried, the bacon flavor giving the fish a very special goodness. This all tastes best if sage brush ashes blow in, and they always do. After much hiking, food like this was a real banquet. It always seemed that every meal that we cooked out was just a little better than the one before. After the meal and a little rest, we were ready to go some more. If no one was in a hurry to get home, we made the most of the day by cooking another meal before starting back to town. Again our appetites were to the point where we could eat a bear long before we started to cook supper.

When everything was ready, we each found a nice rock, hoping that it would not be too hard. The rocks were all placed in a circle around the fire. Everybody filled his plate to overflowing and each, in turn, went to his rock to take a seat at another wonderful meal. For a while, everybody was very quiet, but all of a sudden, somebody had an empty mouth and burst into song. After a little singing and a few hair-raising stories, somebody decided that it was getting late and that we should start home.

Monday was a blue Monday, because we had eaten too much or had hiked too far. My three-room apartment seemed much too small after hiking over acres and acres of land the day before.

Now after people put in a full day at our place, I know just how they will feel the next day. But there is something about being out along a stream with a fishing rod getting tangled up in brush, putting squirming worms on a hook, and coming home so tired that one says, "Never again," and all we hope for is another chance, and again we are out. But this does not appeal to everybody. Some people would be drastically miserable if they had to do this. I have quite a time trout fishing; I am usually a little late. I get such a scare when a trout so unexpectedly hits my bait that I jump instead of pulling.

I like that nibble that the catfish gives. I guess I am a fish-a-woman. I am like an old colored mammy in Texas who said, "Missie, I can sit waiting all day for a fish to come nibble at my bait." That's the way to fish. Take all day, if necessary. The only trouble in Wyoming is that we may not get a mess of fish in one summer. Here the saying is "If summer comes on Sunday, we will go fishing." So here we have to trout fish so we can do it in a hurry.

For me, summers go too fast regardless of what I do. When St. Peter says, "Come, Julie," I will probably be asking for time to do an unfinished job. I wonder if summer is not too short for the wild animals? I see beaver working on a dam as if they had to complete it by a given time. It must be disgusting to them to have people watch them work. The one giving the signal always seems to be trying to get rid of people. It's amazing how well animals can judge the weather. We can tell how bad a snowstorm will be by watching how many pinecones the squirrels store at one time. If they store just a few at a time, winter will be open, but when they store a great quantity in the fall, we know that the snow will be deep. They make their cache by logs or at the trunk of a tree where they can burrow into hollow roots, where, on bad days, they stay and feed. On nice days, we see them sitting on the top of the snow near their cache, eating nuts out of the cone. At harvest time, they go up into a pine tree and throw down many cones at one time, and then they come down and pile the cones up—and then they go up again. They keep this up until they all have the food that they want. Sometimes I pass under a tree just in time to get a thump on my head with a cone.

Squirrels—like birds—have their territories, and other squirrels are not to cross these boundaries. One day, I watched a squirrel steal cones from a pile and take the loot a distance away to another pile when, all of a sudden, a squirrel came down out of a tree where it had been cutting off and throwing down cones. It gave the thief such a thrashing, while chattering like an angry person. Finally, it went back to work.

There are, no doubt, lazy animals, just as there are lazy people. I can truthfully say that I enjoy working. Sure, I would like a vacation once in a while, but I would not like to be deprived of working. My Popeye muscles sometimes get a little overworked and ache, but I am becoming accustomed to hard work. Now, I can hold out for a longer day. Because we work, our life is not all dull.

Our summers are most exciting and enjoyable. New people are constantly coming up. They come because they are in the mood for a good time. They want to get away from things they see and do every day. Here, if they want to burst into song, or turn a handspring out in the yard, they can. The neighbors will not be disturbed, for they live miles away. If someone just wants to sit under a tree and rest, this, too, is permissible. In the evening, we start up the electrical music box and set out an amplifier at each end of the electrically lighted yard, and there is dancing. And in another part of the yard, little children play games. Many times, before the evening is over, either the adults are playing games with the children, or the children are dancing with the adults. No one is told what they can or cannot do. As long as there is no annoyance, everyone can have a good time in his or her own way.

The assembly youngsters, too, have dancing in the yard. After supper, and while they are waiting to go to campfire, the girls in their colorful dresses, flying around like butterflies and the boys in their blue jeans and bright shirts, dancingly sparkle like raindrops in a brilliant sun. Campfire, educational and entertaining in its beautiful setting, is more like a dream than a reality. In a bright full moon, the rugged country around, dancing in the flicker of the campfire, throwing shadows buffonishly, enchantingly delightful and in line, a cross, a campfire, a minister, and to make the scene still more beautiful, one evening my Wopsy came and kissed the minister's hand as he stood before the cross and campfire.

During snowy winter days as I work, before my eyes are pictures of summer. Unconsciousness takes over, and I again live over many months of pleasure. As I throw out hay to the stock on a frosty morning, I do not see the pressed flowers as hay, but as they stood beautiful in the meadow and as they fell before the sickle on a hot summer day. As I mix the beauty of the snow with the beauty of a summer flower, life never gets monotonous.

On special days, such as Thanksgiving, Christmas, and New Year's, we have neighborly gatherings and dinners. And there are birthdays. When our snow weasel was in operation, we could always get out during winter. By spring, we had a packed trail up in the treetops, but the old weasel kept waddling along. If we had a dinner party after our road was snowed in, Otto took the weasel down the road and came back up loaded with people. When he drove into the yard, heads were sticking out of every opening, and everybody was having a wonderful time. I almost cry my eyes out now when we have deep snow, because the weasel is not in operation. We need new dolly wheels and new tracks, which we cannot get, so the weasel is resting under the trees, and we mush snow up to our ears and wish the old machine was on its feet.

6

THE BIG BLIZZARD

On January 1, 1949, we had a dinner party at our place. The folks all went home early, because there was a storm brewing. By morning, the storm hit as if someone had opened a million doors from the North Pole. As Otto started out to feed the stock, I stood in front of the cottage window looking after him, his cap pulled down over his ears, his hands in his coat pockets, bracing himself against the wind.

He had gone only a short distance when he stopped completely, because there was an extra strong gust of wind, and the snow was blinding. I did not see him at all, and again, I saw a dim image. Then the wind seemed to be even stronger, and I could see nothing but a terrific blizzard.

The Winter Cottage After The Big Blizzard

Although Otto had gone only a few feet, he had faded completely from my sight, and by contrast, the snow swept before my eyes like a sea.

I visualized people—old people, young people, children playing. They were all in the yard before my eyes. Some were admiringly looking at the scenery all around. Teasingly, a boy, running across the yard and holding in his hand a tiny green grass snake, tried to frighten some young girls. I heard music coming from the lodge. Gaiety filled the air, and people were dancing and singing.

As the snow was being whipped before my eyes, I saw cars drive into the yard. People were coming out of them on both sides, throwing up a hand in greeting, asking, "Where do we live this time?" I waved back to them and went over to tell them what cabin I had ready for them. They drove over to their temporary home. They carried boxes of food into the cabin. Some strung up fishing rods, yet others crossed the yard, spade in one hand, a tin can in the other one. They were going to dig worms for fish bait.

And I saw young people grouped on green grass, under trees, and on the cottage porch. Each group had an instructor in its midst, teaching them the Golden Rule. I saw a priest crossing the yard, wearing his cassock. He was going to the Goons Grotto. In a little while, I saw another priest … and another one … and this time there were young people with him. They were all going to morning services, and the camp was very quiet. In no time, I heard voices coming from the Grotto. Services were over, and everybody was coming to breakfast. I saw beautiful flowers in the meadow, and I heard the song of many birds. I saw people praying at a little altar under the trees, and I saw a dead cow—many of them. I heard the bark of a wonderful dog … and another one.

All of this mingled before my eyes with the flying snow. I heard a noise, and I saw little deer and lambs running across the porch, and I became conscious. I could no longer see little deer and lambs, but I heard and saw a terrific blizzard.

I looked at the clock. It was almost noon, and Otto was not yet back from feeding the stock. I wondered, "Should I put on my snow clothes and go see if something has happened to him?" I waited a while and tried to figure out how long it would take him to go the quarter of a mile in a blizzard as bad as this—and how long it would take to clean the snow out of the water hole. It must have had at least four feet of snow in it. I looked again, and I saw a dim figure of a man. This time, he was coming with the wind and almost running, but he was trying to hold himself back.

He stepped up on the porch, turned his coat collar down, shook his shoulders to knock some of the snow from his coat, and he was finally in the house, snow packed into his clothes. He was chilled through from the intense cold.

My Topsy and Wopsy were caught out in this blizzard. They weathered it, but when they came home in the spring, they were only partly tame, because they had been out too long with their wild comrades.

The ranchers in our vicinity had enough feed for their stock, but to feed them where they could get the benefit of the feed was a problem. If stock was fed on a hill, where the snow was being blown away, the feed, too, blew away, and the cold was so intense up there that the stock could not stay there to eat, so everyone was trying to feed in sheltered places. But the wind blew everywhere, drifting snow and packing it into the poor critters' hair, chilling them to the bone.

They shivered and tried to eat. They got some of the feed—enough to keep them going. The water, too, was a problem, for it was buried deep under several feet of snow. The stock was thirsty. They crowded into the water hole even before it was shoveled out. A rancher in our vicinity found one of his cows trampled to death in a water hole that had been opened the day before. The poor critter went down to get a drink and was knocked down by other thirsty cattle, and before she could get up and out of the deep snow, she was walked on. More and more thirsty cattle kept coming, trampling over her helpless body, and more and more snow kept covering her, until by the time all of the cattle had their thirsts quenched, life was completely trampled out of her body. The next day, when again the water hole was being cleaned out, her body was found by her owner, and another loss had to be chalked down, but the heartache was there for a long time, knowing a critter had to suffer and die in this manner.

But life must go on. We cannot give up at a time like this. Just a little neglect or carelessness would mean more losses, and it no doubt would cause a hardship. Day in and day out and into the night, people were out tending to their stock, forgetting the pain they themselves suffered. Though some had frozen faces or hands and even frozen feet, they kept going. A good stockman will himself suffer to take care of his stock. This storm lasted for over a month. People had to go out in it; they had to take chances.

There were no life losses in our immediate vicinity, but I believe this was due to people working with the conditions and not against them. Life is secure if we try to make it so, and there is all manner of help for us, but first we must try to help ourselves. Winter and its ruthlessness have been so for centuries. We choose to live where it is more severe; we must accept its cruelties and ugliness and become accustomed to its dealings and its sudden changes and prepare ourselves accordingly.

If a storm is brewing, why take unnecessary chances? Only in an emergency would this be necessary, and should the storm be severe enough, we may even then create a greater emergency. I am beginning to feel that I am a part of it all, and if I work with conditions in which I live and not against them, no undue harm will come to me. We can use the wilderness rightly—take it for its hideousness, vicissitudes, and turbulence and see in it the wonders, thrills, beauties, and marvelous propagation.

We have made trips to and from the ranch with packs on our backs so heavy that we did not think it possible to make the next hill, but conditions were such that only by walking down while the snow was crusted enough to hold us up could such a trip be made.

TOPSY AND WOPSY COMING HOME AFTER THE BIG BLIZZARD

But either we or the stock had to have food, and it made such a trip necessary.

One year, we were out of feed. Snow kept coming. There was no grazing for the stock. Each day, Otto walked down to the ranch and brought up enough grain on his back to feed each critter a little so that they could keep alive until the snow thawed and they could go out to pick up what they could find to eat. Dealing with conditions up here for more than twenty years, we have learned how to make the most of a situation. Not having had any bad accidents and working with logs under dreadful conditions must prove that we have taken precautions. This is no place for casualties, especially during winter.

Every state in the union has its loveliness, its ugliness, its possibilities, its drawbacks, its courageous people, and its cowards. If it were not so, there would be paradise or hell. There is an opportunity for everybody who wants to make it so.

7

WINTER TRAVEL

We were now in a cycle of bad winters. Going after mail on horseback was always a hard trip. Many times, we did not get down for weeks due to continuous blizzards. After the snow got really deep, Otto was elected to the job of going after the mail. He had to carry a shovel on the saddle so that he could dig Lady out of the snow when she got high centered.

It was always an all-day trip when they went to the post office, which was seven miles from our place and farther than we now go. During World War II, we lost our post office, and the mail was put on a route that comes up from Glenrock on Tuesday, Thursday, and Saturday. Weather permitting, people in this part of the country are very nice to anyone making a trip in bad weather. A person is always invited in to eat and to feed his horse.

When asked in to eat, there are two rules one must obey. One is to feed the horse before coming in to eat, and the other one is that, after a meal is finished, each person takes the dishes they have used into the kitchen, scrapes them, and neatly stacks them. This puts one in good standing with the hostess. We had to learn how to live in this part of the country; this was all so different from what I was accustomed to.

When I did not know as much about canning as I now do, I was a little afraid to can meat, so for that reason, we did not always have meat on hand. One winter, we needed meat badly; Otto got the neighbor at the ranch to pick up some fresh meat for us when he made a trip to town. It was all arranged that the meat would be at the ranch in about a week, so one morning very early, Otto started down after it. Going would be hard due to much snow, but the weather was not improving, and the snow was deeper by the day. If we were to have meat, Otto would have to go down at once.

On Teddy's Hill, the snow always drifts to the depth of several feet, and the drift is many feet long, and there is no way of getting around it. A horse cannot go through it. When Otto started down, I went with him to Teddy's Hill; we shoveled a trail through this big drift for Lady to go through. If the wind stayed down, and Otto hurried back, he might get through without again having to shovel.

By the time Otto got to the ranch, he and the horse were both tired, and while he was there, a terrific blizzard blew in from the North. Otto knew that if he did not start back at once, he would have no trail, so he packed the hundred pounds of meat. It had the honor of riding in the saddle, while Otto walked, leading Lady. (Now when Otto went down, the shovel was always stuck into the gun scabbard.)

He got only a short distance from the ranch, and the blizzard grew worse by the minute. By now, the trail that he had made going down was completely drifted in, and wind whipped snow so that Otto could not tell where the road was. Ever so many times, Lady went down in deep snow and could not get up, because she had no footing.

Otto had to unload the meat, help Lady to her feet, get her through the drift, bring the meat across, put it back on the saddle, and go on to the next hazard. This happened many times over. It took them eight hours to make the four-mile round trip. It got dark, and by now, the blizzard was one of those Wyoming killers. I was afraid to go out in it. I was not sure that Otto had left the ranch, but I knew that if he was on his way home, he would need help in the big snowdrift. Finally, I could not wait any longer; I had visions of him and the horse being stuck in the drift.

I lit the gasoline lantern. I dressed warmly and started up to Teddy's Hill. Before I got there, Otto saw the light and called to me. I would have passed him had he not called. The light mingling with the flying snow made it impossible to see more than a few feet.

They had been in the big drift for a long time. The drifting snow filled the trail as fast as Otto shoveled it out. As he shoveled, he had to keep moving Lady forward. Never had I seen such a bewildered man and horse. They were both plastered with snow. Lady, sweating and floundering in the deep snow, had ice all over her. Under her belly, it was several inches thick and stayed there for days.

When we got to the house, I did not know which of the two I should take care of first. I decided that Otto could sit by the stove and rest while I unsaddled Lady and covered her with a blanket. She was too tired to be watered and fed. While Lady was resting at the kitchen door, I gave Otto some hot coffee. I went round and round, from one to the other, thinking that both would die of pneumonia before morning if I did not take good care of them. But, the next morning, outside of being tired, there was no bad effect in man or horse.

We now had many irons in the fire. When we got home from our trapline, if we had a few minutes, we dashed out and put up a few logs on the Goons Grotto, which then had only a good start. Every time we went out to work, we first had to sweep the snow from the logs and walls so that the log being put up would not slip and crush us. Otto had some irons made that we called "iron men," because they helped us so much to hold the logs. This is a piece of iron about three feet long, sharpened to a point at each end and bent down four inches at each end, making two legs on the iron. We drove one iron man on each side of the wall log, making a cradle for the log being put up to lie in while it was being fitted and nailed. We learned to depend on our iron men to such an extent that we would have been lost on a log job without them.

When we were laying up logs, we each had a specific job. I notched the log that was already up, riding the wall from start to finish. Otto picked out the next log to go up, trimming it and notching it while it was still on the ground. When it was laid up, the notch that he made fit into the one that I made. We must have looked like two ants handling those huge logs. They were much larger than we were and outweighed us by several hundred pounds.

I like to sit by an anthill and watch ants work. They seem so well organized.

There were times when a snow weasel would have been a godsend—like a time when I was called to Texas because my mother had had a slight stroke. It was winter, and snow was deep all the way into town. The four miles from our place to the neighbors' ranch were impossible to horseback travel. Otto had been walking down after the mail. By going very early in the morning, the snow was crusted enough to hold him up. At the ranch, he borrowed a horse to ride to the mailbox. By moving fast, he could make it back home before the crusted snow softened.

On one such trip, he came home with a message saying that my mother was sick, and I should go to see her. Though it was a slight stroke, she could have another one that could be fatal. This was World War II. Travel was restricted. If I went, the trip would be hard all the way. I felt that I should go, but just the thought of the trip made me sick all over. But I decided to try it. First, I would have to take care of things at home so that Otto could get along while I was away. I baked a dozen loaves of bread and two large cakes.

I put all of this into an unheated room to freeze. Otto could bring in and thaw out what he needed as he needed it. Otherwise, this would keep until the weather warmed up. I left home sometime in March. I would be gone about a month. Weather up here changes very rapidly. When we start out, we must always be prepared for the worst, so we always start out dressed warmly. Now that the mail came by route, we had to stand out in the open to wait for the postman. Because of the bad roads, we never knew when he would be along. The end of our route where we meet the mail is on one of the worst windswept hills in Wyoming. To stand there on a cold day is like being in a quick freeze, so we try not to get there too early.

I decided that I should start my trip from home on a Monday and go as far as the ranch the first day, stay there overnight, and have plenty of time the next morning to catch the postman. The folks could tell me what time the postman had been coming up.

Monday morning, when we got up, there was a Chinook wind blowing. It was doubtful if the snow would hold me up. Otto insisted on walking down with me, but we had a sick cow. I told him that the cow needed him more than I did, and I could see no reason why he should go down since he would have to come back before dark. I said that I would be down at the ranch before the snow had a chance to soften.

Otto walked with me to Teddy's Hill. From there, the road was all downhill. I could make it. I had on my snow clothes, a scotch cap, mittens, and galoshes that were much too heavy. I carried a cowhide handbag with all of my things packed in it that I would need when I got into civilization.

I had gone about a mile and a half when I started breaking through. I stayed on top of the snow for a few steps, and down I went up to my waist. To get out, I had to put down all of my things and come out on my hands and knees. This I repeated over so many times that when I finally got to a cow trail, I was glad that God made cows.

It took me most of the day to make the four miles, which ordinarily I could make in an hour. That night, I had more aches and pains than a broken-down horse. The next morning, the temperature was down to zero, and a high wind was blowing. I decided to go to the mailbox; when I got there, the postman had not been that far yet, so I kept on going down the road.

I had gone only a short distance when I met a rancher driving a tractor with a box on the back. He was taking his children to school. The children in the box were covered with a heavy quilt to keep warm and dry. He told me to wait. As soon as he unloaded his precious cargo, he would be back. I could ride in the box, and he would take me as far as his place, about six miles down the road.

He was back in no time. I got into the box, pulled the quilt over my head, and away we went. I soon found out why the cover-up business. Those tractor wheels with chains on were really slinging the snow.

When we got to his place, he said that he would take me to the next ranch, but knowing his hungry cattle were waiting to be fed, I would not listen to it. I went in to say hello to the missus, and again I was on my way. I had now long passed the end of the mail route. I kept hoping that I would meet the postman so that I would know if I could ride into town with him or if I would have to walk the rest of the way. Every place I stopped, I was unrecognized.

In the first place, I was too far from home in such deep snow to be me—and dressed like I was, so who could recognize me? And every place I stopped, I was told that the postman had not been getting through. The wind was now blowing a gale. As fast as the ranchers threw hay out to the stock, the wind took it and rolled it across the pasture like a bunch of wild animals running.

My next stop was The Fred Grant ranch. The missus there said that the postman had been as far as their place on the last mail day, but she did not know if he would be up this day, as now was long past his time. The road was badly drifted in the canyon, but if he did not come, they would see that I got to Glenrock.

It was noon when the postman finally came. He was on horseback and was leading a packhorse. He stopped at Grant's long enough to eat and get a fresh horse to ride to the end of the route. When he got back, I asked him if I could ride his packhorse down. He did not have much outgoing mail. I could ride the packhorse. Everybody was being so nice to me, and I felt like an intruder. Here we got a saddle for the packhorse.

We each took part of the mail. The postman tied my handbag on his saddle, and we were on our way. It was now well into the afternoon, and a high zero wind was still blowing; we had a twenty-mile ride ahead of us (if I could stay on the horse that long).

The horses were willing to travel, since they were going home. Where the snow was not too deep, they took right down the road. After being fed and rested at the ranch, they were really peppy. Before we got down through the canyon, I knew that my horse thought he was carrying a dead elephant, for I was simply numb from the cold. All I could do was hang onto the saddle horn.

We had traveled about fifteen miles when we saw a car parked on the road. In the car was my brother-in-law waiting for me. When we stopped at the car, I came off the horse like a dead cow. I was simply stiff from riding in a cold wind. The only bad effect that I had from the trip was a frozen neck on one side and a sore spot where I sat.

Now I had a long train ride ahead of me. The next day, my sister took me to Douglas. From there, I would start my train journey. In Douglas, I was told that I could not get a Pullman to Denver, and if my seat was needed for a serviceman, I would have to give it up.

In Denver, I tried to get a Pullman to Fort Worth, as by then I just could not see how I could stay alive if I did not put that carcass of mine down on a bed to rest. In Denver, I was again told, "No Pullman for civilians," but if I was going to be around, I should come to the ticket window at intervals. If something did show up in the line of a Pullman seat, I could have it provided that a serviceman did not want it. I pestered that poor ticket agent so much that all I had to do was look at him, and he shook his head no. But right at the last minute, when I again looked at him, he motioned to me to come to the window. He said that he had a lower berth. It had been reserved for a patient to be moved from a hospital who, at the last minute, could not be moved. So somebody's misfortune was my fortune, and I had a lower berth to Fort Worth.

I went to bed early, and I slept until I was wakened by a hand pulling my feet and a voice saying, "Fort Worth." Had someone told me that I could sleep so many hours without waking up, I would not have believed it. It is a good thing a serviceman did not want that berth. The only way he could have gotten me out of it would have been to drag me out and drop me in the runway.

When I got out of the train at Fort Worth, the depot was jammed with people. I did not know that there could be that many soldiers anyplace other than a battlefield. The streets were also jammed. Every taxi said, "Reserved for servicemen." I did not mind walking to the other depot, for now I needed a little exercise. I was on the last leg of my journey. When I finally reached my destination, my mother was at the station to meet me, and of the two of us, she looked the better.

Dropping from eight thousand feet in elevation to almost sea level was a little too much for me. I wanted to sleep day and night. At the end of three weeks, I had such a strong urge to go home that I was no longer enjoying my visit, so I told my mother that I was going home. She was surprised at my sudden decision, but she felt that I knew what I wanted to do.

The next day, I was on my way home. The train trip home was the worse of the two. Between Fort Worth and Denver, there was hardly standing room, and the heat was terrific. I was really happy to see the mountains. From Denver, I wired my sisters to meet me in Douglas so that I could catch our postman on his next trip up our way. I made it by the skin of my teeth. When we got to end of the route (by car this time) on that windswept hill, I met the worst ground blizzard that I was ever in. I could hardly stand up when I got out of the car, and I am not sure that I would have started out walking to The Robbins ranch had it not been for one of the young girls from the ranch coming after the mail. She was riding bareback and could not take me and all of my paraphernalia, so she hurriedly rode home and came back with a saddle horse for me to ride. After several attempts of trying to get on the horse, I finally got between the two horses, and I managed to get on without being blown over on the other side. I no more than hit the saddle and the horse took out for home like he was moonstruck.

GOING AFTER MAIL. ON TEDDY'S HILL. OTTO, LADY AND TEDDY NUMBER TWO.

I didn't want to be out in this blizzard anymore than he did, but I did think he should have at least given me a chance to sit down on my long coattail. Sailing through the air, my coat stood out straight behind me like a pigeon's tail.

And history says that Paul Revere made a fast, heroic ride. That boy was practically standing still in my comparison. I was so very happy to get down from that horse and so very thankful for having had him to ride, but I did think he should have cut the throttle a little.

The folks at the ranch were surprised to see me back so soon, and they insisted that I stay and have dinner before starting to walk home from their place. The storm blew itself out as suddenly as it came up, but the sky was still overcast. While we were eating, who came in but Otto! He, too, was surprised to see me, and I was surprised and glad to see him. He had no idea that I would be home, but I am sure that he was a little happy to see me.

Just as soon as we'd finished eating, we started home. Walking on the snow this time was not as bad, because it now had a hard crust. We were home in a little more than an hour. The sky was still very heavily overcast, but the wind had died down completely. In the night, it started snowing so hard that everything was like a sheet hanging before one's eyes.

The next morning, April 13, we had five feet of fresh snow. Had I stayed in town overnight, I would have been stuck there for three weeks with Otto at home alone. So that was the urge that kept pulling me home.

Looking out the next morning, it was unbelievable that so much snow could fall in one night. All of the fence posts around the yard were out of sight, and the out of doors looked as if it was smothering, covered with all of the whiteness.

We had to get to the winter barn. Otto said that he was sure we would find two new calves there. Lady was in the barn with the cows. We each took a shovel that we always keep on the porch during winter for a time just like this. When I stepped into the snow, I felt like I was in a sea. I couldn't go anyplace. Otto stepped to the edge of the porch and started shoveling snow, throwing it from side to side and inching his way toward the barn, and I was right behind him. When he could shovel no more, I took over. By noon, we had made the quarter of a mile to the barn. Upon our arrival, we found the two new calves, but one had chilled to death. The other one was all right.

But now, we were only at the barn. We still had to go to the haystack, which was about half the distance we had come so far, but now we had good old Lady to help us break trail. It took all of the strength and endurance that we both had to take care of the stock. I was so glad that I'd made it home before the storm came so that I could help Otto so that he would not have to go through it alone. I got on Lady and slowly pushed through the deep snow to the haystack. My legs dragged in the snow and piled it on Lady's back. Little by little and only a few steps at a time, we finally made it to the haystack. Otto followed in Lady's tracks.

After resting for a while, Otto made up bundles of hay, which I took to the cows on Lady. They got only enough to keep them going. Later, they could have more.

The wind blew just enough to fill our trails as fast as we made them. After a week, the snow was settling, and in another week, we had packed trails. Finally, we were back to normal. Winters then were harder. Now we have less snow but more wind—but we can get around better in a wind than we can in deep snow. So let it blow.

Wyoming winters are not new to Otto. In his young days, he was quite the cowboy. A bellhop in one of the large Milwaukee hotels, he suddenly decided to become a cowboy. Rigging himself out in a pair of bright red boots, he started for Wyoming. As soon as he stepped from the train in Glenrock, it was evident that "Boots" had come to town. From then on, he was known as Boots Bruns.

His first job was on his uncle's ranch, going out on fall roundup for months at a time with nothing to call home but the old chuck wagon, but at the end of a long, hard day, it was a welcome sight to the cowboys. This meant good food, a few songs, and a little wild storytelling before rolling up into a blanket for the night under the stars. They would again roll out at the crack of dawn and ride all day after wild cattle.

The chuck wagon followed right along with the roundup, and each day had three hot meals ready for the boys—unless a bucking bronco came right through the kitchen setup and scattered pots and pans to the four winds and a good meal was lost. And the wagon cook came out shaking his fists, cursing and kicking at what was left of his kitchen.

By now, the wild cayuse was gone, but still kicking trying to ungear himself. Each cowboy had from seven to eleven horses that he used and cared for, some of which were only partly saddle broke. When a cowboy had to use one of those green horses, as soon as he applied his seat to the saddle, the horse was on its way. As a rule, those half-broke horses were used on night herd, which meant that some of the boys had to be put out riding all night, not going anyplace in particular, but only keeping watch so the rounded-up cattle did not again stray away. On this job, the boys had more time to finish breaking the green horses.

The boys, no doubt, enjoyed this work. One can always hear them say, "Those were the good old days." Now in Wyoming, roundup days are no longer general. Most ranch lands are fenced in, and stock is grazed on this territory. However, the large outfits have their own roundup. They go out early in the fall to bring in beef for shipping and again later to bring in what cattle are in poor condition and would have to have special care. And I suppose still later, if snow is too deep for good grazing, there is a general roundup, and all stock is fed.

How so many cattle can all be found over hundreds of acres of land so rugged that to penetrate it seems impossible is hard to understand, but I guess the boys make many trips each year over the territory assigned to them, and finally they know every rock and every nook. I would not make a stockwoman. I would want to house all of my stock during a blizzard. I could not stand the thought of letting stock that had made it possible for me to have a comfortable house and a warm bed to sleep in stay out in weather so bad that many do not live through it—or the thought of little calves coming into a cold world with no shelter.

Up here, we have no set rule. We cannot say definitely that we will do a certain job at a certain time. During summer, things pop up that we least expect. If we have a breathing spell when we do not have to serve meals to guests and the hay is ready to be cut, I dash out and help Otto put it up. Many times right in the middle of a big job, people come up, and I have to leave Otto to struggle alone, but somehow, we eventually get the job done. After the hay is out of the way, we must start getting in winter wood. This, too, we do a little at a time, but if we have wood down on the ground, it does not spoil like cut hay will if not stacked and then cured. For this reason, the hay is our big problem.

After all of the wood is hauled in, we can cut it up anytime. Having a power saw, we can cut up enough wood in two days to last us for six months. During summer, we use about as much wood as we do during winter. Some days there are seven ranges going all day and well into the night.

After the wood is in, we start hauling up winter supplies, and by Thanksgiving, we must have everything up that we will need for the winter without notice and at no certain time of year. If the road is still open to car travel after Thanksgiving, fine, and if it is snowed in, fine, too. Then we just settle down into our little world and busy ourselves with the many jobs that we must do to keep the place from falling apart.

Every tool must be picked up that has been left here and there during summer, and all of these things must be put into a special place so that when we need them, we can find them. A chain, shovel, or an axe left on the ground would be snow covered in no time, and we could not find them until next summer. And winter is when such things are most needed. When working on a job—summer or winter—we never come home leaving our tools on the job, because we never know if we will be going to the same job the next day, or if there will be something more urgent that we must do first.

The cold is now hard on Otto, so I took over the job of feeding the stock. The temperature has been down to thirty-five below zero, and for days, it did not go above twenty below zero. Going to feed on cold mornings, Rex felt the cold more than I did. Crying a little, he would sit in the snow, first holding up one paw and then the other one, looking up at me as though he were surprised that I did not hold my feet up and cry, too.

We have such understanding animals. This morning, Tommy jumped up on Otto's ore chest and upset it; when it hit the floor, all of the 216 samples flew out of their little boxes, and there was a mess on the floor. Now Otto is sitting in the middle of the floor on some newspapers, and he is trying to put all of the samples into their specific boxes. This chest is a strong box affair with two trays. Each tray has 108 tiny, open-face boxes, and in each box, a piece of ore (rock to me) and each sample has a number that is supposed to be stuck on the ore, but over many years of use, many of the numbers came off and were in the bottom of their little boxes. Now, Otto is looking for little pieces of paper about the size of a match head, and he is trying to associate each with a specific piece of rock. He is having what seems like a little trouble. He is talking partly to himself and partly (I hope) to Tommy, because I would rather that what he is saying be meant for Tommy than me. Although I had nothing to do with upsetting the sample chest, I did pick up poor Tommy when he was just a kitten, and I gave him to Otto. Otto likes yellow cats.

Now, as Otto sits in the middle of all of this mess—open mineral books in front of him, out of which he is trying to identify the samples of which he is not sure—angelic Tommy sits looking at him. Occasionally, he goes over to rub his whiskers on Otto and to say how sorry he is that Otto did not put the chest far enough on its bench so that it could not fall off. After all, Tommy has to sit in front of the window and look out. He has nothing else to do. The weather is too bad to go hunting.

At our house, we are all a bunch of old maids. We each have our specific place. This goes for Rex, too. Our winter quarters, when finished, will be the living-dining rooms in our new house, but now the rest of the house is still under construction, so we use this part, which is finished inside with wallboard and painted. This part is my homestead cabin. When we rebuilt it, we made a large opening in the partition, so now the two rooms are more like one room. This is the arrangement. One part has a range in it and is the kitchen. The other part has a circulator heater and a rug on the floor and is our bedroom-living room. In the heater side of the room is the living room part. The heater is four feet from the wall, a fact that does not seem important, but really it is, because here much disturbance takes place.

Directly behind the heater and against the wall is a deerskin rug, which is Rex's own property and where he can sleep on really cold days or nights. On each side of his bed is a straight chair. One is for each, Otto's and my many coats, caps, mittens and the many other things we must put on before we go out, and which Rex watches to such extent that a cat gets a beating if it as much as looks at one of the chairs. One side of the heater is Otto's corner, and the other corner is where I live. In my corner, I have a desk and a straight chair, and between the desk and stove, I have a chaise lounge that I made—and if I do say it myself, it is the most comfortable piece of furniture that we own.

In this chair, I spend all of my winter evenings. Otto has a desk, too, but his is an old one and was built when real wood was put into furniture. Therefore, it stays in the summer house, because it is too heavy to be moved. My desk is also made out of wood, but I think the wood was pressed into paper before it was made into a desk. Just the same, it's new, and it's a desk. Otto has his corner, his favorite rocking chair and he uses my sewing machine for a table, and in Otto's corner are two orange crates where magazines and books are pigeon-holed, and the sample chest on its bench, I hope.

When Otto wants to sit in his chair, he first has to move Tommy or Skeezix, and he puts them on my chaise lounge. When I want to sit down, I first have to push them off on the floor, and I no more than sit down, and they sit right on top of me. The only time I am rid of at least one of the cats is when Otto is tired of sitting, and he starts walking around the table, which is partly in the kitchen and partly in the living room, and it is long enough that a few rounds gives Otto plenty of exercise. As soon as he starts walking, it makes no difference how soundly Skeezix is sleeping—he jumps down from his bed and starts to walk right behind Otto. When Otto stops, Skeezix runs in front of him and wants to be picked up and carried, so Otto picks him up, and Skeezix is carried around the table a few times.

This he would not miss for the world and which really looks cute, Otto walking, carrying Skeezix in his arms. But Skeezix is a pretty cat. He is more black than white, and on his nose is a crazy black blotch. This makes him look like he has a dirty face, but no one could accuse Skeezix of that, because he is the most out washingest cat in the country.

Besides the two corners, the rest of the house we all occupy. I take my exercise when I go feed the six cows and calves and Lady. I go to the haystack on one side of Meadow Creek. After I have fed and opened the water hole, I go to the winter barn, and I clean out what the stock dropped during the night, and I come home on the other side of the creek. By the time I get home, I have made a horseback trip of a mile. I am not trapping this winter. I am just being lazy sitting at my desk and pushing a pencil. During winter, our day starts at 7:00 a.m. Otto starts fires in the two stoves, and when the chill is out of the house, I get up. I dress and put on a face (this gives me a lift) and comb my hair, and I get breakfast. Otto makes the bed and here, too, his helper is on the job. Skeezix has so much fun trying to tear the bed up as fast as Otto is trying to make it, so Otto gives up, and he makes the bed while Skeezix eats his breakfast.

While I feed, Otto puts the rest of the house in order. In the evening, we have our big meal, and we wash the dishes that were stacked after breakfast and lunch. We acquired this habit when soap was scarce. During summer, I am good to Otto. I start the fire in the cookstove, feed the chickens, and prepare breakfast while Otto takes two extra winks. He says it's nice to get up in the morning, but he likes to stay in bed.

Spring days are hectic. One day, it's zero, and the next, it is forty or more above. My heavy overshoes by now are too heavy, because I have been mushing snow in them too long, and my legs are tired. We put on clothes and take them off, because we either are too hot or too cold.

The cows get their bags snow-burnt, and when we try to milk them, they kick us to Kingdom Come if we do not jump quickly enough.

THE SNOW WEASEL, BUCKING SNOW

Just when I thought everything was peaceable, I get knocked over. It's always my luck to land into something soft, and I think, "Phew! What am I sitting in?" I see red, but I am really green.

An early fisherman wants to know why the creek channel is so yellow where it has cut through the ice, and I say, "That's where I scorched the ice when I was ice skating on my fanny."

The wood is too wet to burn, and I have to say things that don't sound good, so I pray a little, and I pucker my lips up and blow into the fire, and by the time I am ready to start breakfast, I am the worst mess anyone could hope to see.

Summers are different. It seems that all I do is mess around in water. I am either washing clothes, dishes, or dirty feet. Otto and I eat our breakfast together in the kitchen. As soon as we have swallowed the last bite, we rush out to milk, and I hope that all of the guests will sleep until the milking is done and the milk is separated. I hope that I have had time to clean up the milk things and myself before I have to start breakfast for them. I tell everybody the night before that if they don't stay in bed until eight o'clock, they may have to cook their own breakfast.

8

Winter in Town

The fall of 1953 was the bad one. Because of Otto's failing health, we were compelled to leave the mountains for the winter. After twenty years, life in town would be hard for us all. Lady started out with us, and she, too, would have to be considered. Rex was now gone, but we had Chico. We sold all of the stock but two milch cows and two calves. Skeezix and Tommy were also with us.

The stock would be trucked to Glenrock; the other animals would ride in the car with us. I had saved two dozen laying hens for next summer; they, too, would ride in the back end of the car.

With heavy hearts, we started packing things that mice could damage. We now had twenty-two completely made beds, all of the bedding for which would have to be packed away. With my two good mousers and many traps working all winter, it was all I could do to keep mice from chewing things of value; and how could we keep damage down and be away all winter? This was a problem. There are so many things over which man has no control. Old bruin could push in the door and, not finding us home, could do much damage. And not only he, but all manner of creatures could come in to do their share. We do not have to guard against man, but animals. Nature is sometimes cruel, but never deliberately so. Seemingly unimportant little precautions may be of much help in keeping our home from falling apart while we are away.

I tried to think what we would need in town. It seemed foolish to take food down; some things would not keep until spring, so those we would have to take. So we packed and packed until it seemed that we were moving away for good. We started down in November; we could not take a chance on getting snowed in.

Now, settled on the outskirts of town, the cows and Lady were pastured. Lady was very unhappy to be away from her mountain; she had roamed over so much open range that to be in a small pasture was not for her. She stood looking toward her home in the hills. We felt sure that she would not go back in the spring, as now she was twenty-nine years old. Sunday, January 17, 1954, she went to sleep, never again to awaken to go to her mountain home. She had lived with us for twenty-two years. There was never a more understanding horse. She had gone through thick and thin with us; we *loved* her with all our hearts.

Chico was happy in town, but the cats were continually in line for a battle.

Otto was not doing well; he'd had two bad spells of what seemed like indigestion. The doctor could not find the cause of his discomfort. By much talking and coaxing, he went to the veterans hospital in Cheyenne, where he passed away on February, 9, 1954, from a heart condition.

The balance of February and March were trying days. I sold the cows and calves. I now, too, looked toward the mountains, wondering how I could go back alone. But I had no choice.

May, Chico, Tommy, Skeezix, and I piled into the old Ford, and we started back home. Whatever happens to me must also happen to my animals; they depend on me, and I depend on them. I expected to run into a few snowdrifts before I reached home. I managed until I got to Teddy's Hill; there was a drift three feet deep and about twelve feet wide, which I would have to shovel out or leave the car and walk the last mile home. The day was still young; I decided to open the road. I backed the car down the hill, put on chains, and went back up to shovel. The cats and Chico could go hunting while I worked. By late afternoon and after much hard work, I had the snow out of the way. Now I would have to cut spruce branches and put them over the bare ground that I had just uncovered to be sure that I could keep going once I got that far up the hill. I was sure that if I did not make it on the first try, I would be stuck. With a silent prayer, I started up the hill as fast as the old car could go. To my surprise, I made it through, and though I banged a tree, I kept on going. When I got on dry ground, I stopped to pick up my passengers; they were coming as hard as they could run. When they heard the car come up the hill, they knew that we were now going home.

I opened the door, and they jumped in. I had only a short distance to go, and I would be at the last gate and almost home. As soon as I stopped at the gate and opened the door, all of the animals jumped out and started running toward home. I am sure that they thought they would find Otto, for they, too, had missed him.

As I started down the last hill and into the yard, I thought I would die. I could not breathe; I seemed to be suffocating. My heart was never so heavy. Finally, when I drove into the yard, I sat in the car, and I cried and cried. I do not remember how I got into the house or how I got to bed. But that night, I slept from complete exhaustion. I had worked hard all day and had eaten nothing.

My poor animals were so hungry and confused the next morning. "You have changed," they seemed to say. But I have not. I am here as always; only my world has changed. Now I must work alone; I must make decisions alone. Will I make them wisely? Death is cruel. But death is kind when it awakens us to a new return.

For days, I was dazed like a person standing on a state line, leaving one and returning to another. Thrown together into a lovely wilderness where two people depend on one another, life is beautiful. I find myself constantly standing still just to listen to nothing. The sound I hope to hear never comes. I catch myself starting into the house to ask Otto a question. One day, I actually ran to tell him that there were wild turkeys in the yard; he thought he had seen some last fall. If only I could go to the corral and Lady or the cows would be there. The chickens may help when I bring them up.

I cannot run away from this loneliness; I must face it. For three summers, I operated alone. I repaired fences and the many buildings. I drove thirty or forty miles after supplies. I cooked for my guests and did cleaning and washing. During hunting season, I went out with hunters. I had learned to depend on Chico, especially at night; during winter, someone shot him.

Snow was beginning to fly; I would have to take my car to the ranch, as I may be snowed in for winter. I yet had all of the packing to do like the winter before. It had been snowing at my place off and on for days; snow was about two feet deep. I had to complete my arrangements as quickly as possible and snowshoe down.

I had few things that were a must in my life; those I packed into a sack to carry across my shoulders. I would put Tommy and Skeezix into a half-bushel basket and carry them. We would start early the next morning; on snowshoes, the going would be slow and hard. With the heavy load I had to carry, we would be on the road the rest of the day.

The next morning, the sky was overcast. The snow was getting soft, and the going would be hard. I put the cats into their baskets, tied the covers on, and started out. But with every step I took, I sank into the soft snow so deep that I could hardly lift my snowshoes; they were so heavy with snow. The cats were too heavy, too; I could not make it. In desperation, I went back to the house, got the .22 rifle, and, through a hole in the basket covers, I shot first Tommy and then Skeezix. To me, they were not dead cats in the basket; they were my pets, my friends.

Now I had nothing left. I got deathly sick. I could not move. How many more heartaches would there be for me? I could not leave Tommy and Skeezix in the baskets all winter; I buried them alongside my first and second Teddy, and I stumbled my way down to the ranch where I had left the car. Death is cruel. But death is kind when it awakens us to a new return.

9

Final Pages

Many years have passed since Otto and I started building our home together in our valley. The place has completely changed. It now looks like a little village. I feel sure that many people can recall a pleasant and memorable weekend or a month at our place, and I have a feeling that, at least in part, I have accomplished my desire to make people happy, for the proof lies in many returning year after year.

Now, as I have pushed my pencil over many sheets of paper, I have again lived my life over the past twenty-five years. My heart has been glad, and my heart has been sad.

As I now look back over many years of hard work, I feel that if it were all in one pile, I could not believe that two people could have accomplished a task so great. It is all here before my own eyes, although only I can see it, as it is not in one pile, but scattered over 1,288 acres of land. And now, on a beautiful summer day, I am sitting on the thick green grass in my valley, the rugged terrain before my eyes, nature's lovely carpet at my feet. There are mountains on all sides, and their slopes are tree covered. Only their rugged peaks show bare, and there are flowers all around me.

The little creek that once had so much brush on its banks now only has a scattering of large trees for the birds to nest in and for the cows to rest in their shade. The flowers are blue like the sky, rose like a beautiful sunset, white like the winter snow and a symbol of purity, and gold like the sun.

When God decorated his heavenly home, he may have thrown out what paint he had leftover, and the breezes took it and sprinkled it over the hills and over my valley.

I see a mountain canary up in a tree. He looks like he was there when many of the colors fell; his head is bright red, his neck shades into orange, his body a beautiful yellow, and he looks like he went wading in the little creek and forgot to wash the mud from his feet. And there is a blue bird trying to balance himself on a delphinium stalk, fluttering his beautiful blue wings. He looks like he may have been right in the way when God painted the sky.

And all that I see is free. My God is so good to me. He gave me flowers to smell and to see and the birds to sing to me. The sun and the starlight are also free. God made all these, and He gave them to me.

When the day is done, I may not have earthly accomplishments to give in return for the many pleasures I have enjoyed from nature's beauty, but, dear God, I give you my hands. With them, I have earned my living honestly. Now I bury my face into the soft green grass, and I cry. I do not cry for myself, but for the many people whose rulers oppress them and make them slaves, and they are taxed for being slaves, while their rulers sit and count their gold. And they are not yet satisfied, so their slaves must go out and fight a war for them, which they have declared on their weaker neighbor for no reason that's good.

I would not give my humble home for the castle of a ruler or a king, and I would not give up my God, peace, and freedom for all of his wealth and glory.

The only bright lights I know are the stars. The only soft carpet that I have to walk upon is the soft snow. The only noise like that of a big city that I hear is the wind whistling through the trees. I have dreamed of a beautiful home with soft carpets and of the bright lights of the theater and of a visit to a big city, and I would like to travel over every mile of our wonderful America from the most rugged to the most beautiful places, and I would love to visit the country where Jesus lived.

If my rights are trampled upon, I as the [blank] woman upon this earth, and if were [blank], I could fire bullets straight and fast like a good soldier, but if everyone felt the peace and contentment within themselves as I do, we would need no bullets, and there would never be another war.

I am not worthy of the dust from my savior's feet, but I wish I could stand upon the highest mountain with outstretched arms. I wish that I could give myself a twirl, that I could reach into every part of the world, and that I could give to all of the people this wonderful feeling that I have in my heart.

Then we all could live peaceably together in my beautiful world.

The End